THE
ART
OF
PERSPECTIVE

Unlocking Clarity and Purpose in a
Chaotic World

FELIX GRAYSON

MINDSPARK
PUBLISHING

To those who seek clarity in chaos and purpose in the journey—may your perspective illuminate your path and inspire others to find their own.

"We can complain because rose bushes have thorns, or rejoice because thorns have roses."

— *Alphonse Karr*

ABOUT STONED PHILOSOPHER

Welcome to the *Stoned Philosopher* series—where timeless wisdom meets the modern world.

Each book distills powerful lessons from history's greatest minds, leaders, and thinkers—transforming their ideas into practical insights for today's challenges.

From mastering habits, calm, and resilience to understanding success, leadership, and meaning, this collection invites you to think deeper, live wiser, and see life from new perspectives.

Whether you're exploring *Modern Zen*, uncovering *The Wisdom of Warriors*, or seeking clarity through *The Art of Perspective*, every title offers a journey toward self-mastery and understanding.

Discover the full *Stoned Philosopher* collection and more at **FelixGrayson.com**, home of **Mind-Spark Publishing**—where knowledge, philosophy, and storytelling come together to spark lifelong curiosity.

FelixGrayson.com 🔍

Wisdom isn't something we find—it's something we grow into.

Let the journey begin.

CONTENTS

INTRODUCTION: A NEW WAY OF SEEING

Imagine standing on a mountaintop at sunrise. As the first light touches the horizon, the world below begins to reveal itself—rolling hills, winding rivers, and tiny villages, all coming into view. In that moment, everything seems connected, part of a greater whole. This is the gift of perspective: the ability to step back, see the bigger picture, and make sense of the seemingly chaotic landscape of life.

Perspective is not merely about what we see; it is about how we see. It is the lens through which we interpret events, relationships, and even ourselves. While the facts of life may remain the same, our perspective determines how we understand them—whether a challenge feels insurmountable or manageable, whether a relationship feels strained or redeemable, whether life itself feels meaningful or empty.

This book is an invitation to explore the art of perspective: to learn how to shift your lens, un-

cover deeper truths, and unlock clarity and purpose in a chaotic world. It is not about offering
easy answers or rigid frameworks but about
equipping you with tools, insights, and stories
to navigate life with wisdom and intentionality.

The Power of Perspective

Why does perspective matter? At its heart,
perspective shapes the quality of our lives. It
influences how we make decisions, approach
challenges, and connect with others. A clear
and intentional perspective allows us to align
our actions with our values, creating a sense of
coherence and fulfillment.

Conversely, a distorted or limited perspective
can trap us in cycles of frustration, indecision,
and disconnection. Consider how easy it is to
get caught up in the narrow view of a problem,
focusing so intently on its details that we lose
sight of the bigger picture. Perspective frees
us from this tunnel vision, reminding us that
challenges are part of a larger story—one that
we have the power to shape.

History offers countless examples of the transformative power of perspective. Think of Nelson Mandela, who, despite spending 27 years in prison, maintained a perspective of hope and reconciliation that would later heal a divided nation. Or Viktor Frankl, who found meaning in the suffering of a concentration camp and used that perspective to guide others toward purpose. These stories remind us that perspective is not just a tool for survival but a pathway to greatness.

What This Book Offers

In the pages ahead, we will journey through the dimensions of perspective, exploring how it influences every facet of our lives. Each chapter builds on the idea that perspective is a practice—a dynamic and evolving way of engaging with the world.

- We begin by examining **clarity**, the foundation of perspective. How can we strip away distortions and biases to see the world as it truly is?

- Next, we challenge the assumptions and cognitive shortcuts that limit our understanding, learning to expand our viewpoint and embrace complexity.

- We delve into the role of chaos and uncertainty, reframing them as opportunities for growth rather than obstacles to overcome.

- From there, we turn inward, exploring the power of self-awareness and the practice of gaining perspective on ourselves.

- Finally, we examine how perspective shapes our legacy—how the clarity we cultivate can inspire and empower others, creating ripples of impact that extend far beyond our individual lives.

This book draws on timeless wisdom from history's greatest thinkers, modern insights from neuroscience and psychology, and practical strategies for applying perspective in everyday life. Whether you are seeking to overcome a personal challenge, improve your relationships, or simply find greater meaning in your daily routines, these chapters are designed to meet you where you are and guide you forward.

An Invitation to Reflection

As you begin this journey, I invite you to reflect on your own perspective. What lens do you bring to the world? How has it been shaped by your experiences, beliefs, and assumptions? Are there areas where your perspective feels clear and aligned, and others where it feels clouded or constrained?

Perspective is deeply personal, yet it is also profoundly relational. It shapes not only how we see ourselves but also how we see others and the world around us. By examining our perspective with curiosity and compassion, we open the door to growth and transformation.

The Challenges of a Chaotic World

We live in a time of unprecedented complexity and change. The pace of life accelerates with each passing year, fueled by technological advances, global interconnection, and a constant flood of information. This chaos can feel overwhelming, leaving us searching for clarity and direction amidst the noise.

Perspective offers an antidote to this overwhelm.

It helps us navigate uncertainty with resilience and grace, finding meaning even in the midst of disorder. It reminds us that while we cannot control the external world, we can control how we respond to it. By cultivating perspective, we become architects of our own lives, shaping our narrative with intention and clarity.

The Journey Ahead

The chapters of this book are not a map but a guide—a series of waypoints to help you navigate your unique journey. Along the way, you will encounter stories of resilience and transformation, practical exercises for building clarity and intentionality, and reflections to inspire your own growth.

This journey is not about perfection. It is about progress. Perspective is not something we achieve once and for all; it is a practice that unfolds over time. Each step brings new insights, challenges, and opportunities to deepen our understanding.

As you read, I encourage you to approach these pages with an open mind and heart. Take what resonates, experiment with what intrigues you, and reflect on how these ideas might apply to your own life. Perspective is a deeply personal journey, and its rewards are as unique as the individuals who undertake it.

A Final Thought

At the core of perspective is hope—the belief that we have the capacity to grow, to connect, and to create meaning. It is this hope that transforms challenges into opportunities, relationships into sources of strength, and ordinary moments into profound experiences.

As you embark on this journey, know that you are not alone. The wisdom of those who came before you, the support of those around you, and your own inner resilience will guide you forward. Together, they form the foundation of a life lived with clarity, purpose, and intention.

In the words of Marcel Proust, *"The real voyage of discovery consists not in seeking new landscapes, but in having new eyes."* Let this book be an invitation to discover those new eyes—to cultivate a perspective that illuminates your path and empowers you to embrace the fullness of life.

CHAPTER 1: THE LENS OF CLARITY – SEEING THE WORLD AS IT IS

The Concept of Clarity

Clarity is the compass of the mind—a tool that aligns thoughts, emotions, and actions with truth. To define clarity is to grasp its essence as the ability to perceive situations and decisions without distortion, much like observing a landscape through a spotless window rather than one smeared with grime. It is the foundation upon which sound judgment, purposeful action, and meaningful relationships are built. But in a world teeming with noise, distractions, and biases, mental clarity often feels elusive, like sunlight obscured by storm clouds.

The pursuit of clarity begins with understanding its purpose: to see the world as it is, not as we wish or fear it to be. True clarity is not rooted in idealism or cynicism but in objectivity—a quality that demands effort and vigilance. When clarity is present, confusion gives way to confidence, and indecision is replaced by purposeful direction.

Yet, this pristine state of mind is not easily achieved. Our perceptions are constantly shaped by a complex interplay of external influences and internal biases, many of which operate beyond our conscious awareness. Philosophers and thinkers throughout history have grappled with this tension, seeking to unravel the forces that cloud our vision.

The Veil of Bias

The Greek philosopher Epictetus once remarked, *"Men are disturbed not by things, but by the views they take of them."* This statement underscores a fundamental truth: our experiences are not defined by reality itself but by the interpretations we impose upon it. Biases act as veils, coloring our perceptions in ways that often go unnoticed.

Consider confirmation bias—the tendency to seek information that supports pre-existing beliefs while dismissing evidence to the contrary. This cognitive shortcut simplifies the world, reducing the discomfort of uncertainty, but at a steep cost: it narrows perspective and entrenches ignorance. Similarly, emotional biases—such as fear, anger, or attachment—further distort clarity by tethering our thoughts to transient feelings rather than enduring truths.

These biases are not inherently malicious; they are byproducts of a mind evolved to navigate survival rather than truth. Early humans relied on snap judgments to evade predators and seize fleeting opportunities. But in the modern world, where complexity and nuance reign, such mental shortcuts often lead us astray.

The External World: A Storm of Influences

Beyond internal biases, external influences bombard us at every turn. Social media algorithms feed us echo chambers of tailored content, reinforcing existing worldviews and stifling dissent. Advertisements exploit insecurities, subtly reshaping our desires and priorities. Even the well-meaning advice of friends and family can skew our perspective, often reflecting their values rather than our own.

Historical examples illustrate the perils of allowing external forces to dictate perception. During the Salem witch trials of the late 17th century, collective hysteria supplanted rational thought, leading to tragic consequences. The clarity of evidence was drowned in the cacophony of fear and superstition. This episode serves as a stark reminder of the importance of questioning narratives, especially those amplified by collective fervor.

In today's context, the stakes are no less significant. When external influences go unchecked, we risk losing sight of our authentic selves. Clarity, then, becomes an act of resistance—a deliberate choice to pause, reflect, and reclaim the autonomy of our thoughts.

The Emotional Fog

Emotions are both allies and adversaries in the quest for clarity. While they provide valuable insights into our values and desires, they can also cloud judgment when left unexamined. A heated argument, for instance, often reveals how anger narrows focus, spotlighting grievances while eclipsing empathy and solutions.

The Stoics, masters of emotional clarity, advocated for the practice of observing emotions without being consumed by them. Marcus Aurelius, in his *Meditations*, wrote, *"You have power over your mind—not outside events. Realize this, and you will find strength."* This principle invites us to step back from emotional turbulence, much like a sailor navigating a storm, seeking the calm beyond the chaos.

In practice, this means developing emotional awareness—the ability to recognize and name feelings without immediate reaction. It also involves cultivating detachment, not in the sense of apathy, but as a means of preventing emotions from dictating actions.

The Call to See Clearly

To strive for clarity is to embark on a lifelong journey of refining perception and judgment. It requires humility to admit when our views are clouded, courage to confront uncomfortable truths, and discipline to resist the allure of easy answers. Clarity is not a static state but a dynamic process, requiring constant adjustment as new information and experiences arise.

In this quest, clarity becomes more than a mental exercise; it transforms into a way of being. It empowers us to approach challenges with confidence, navigate relationships with authenticity, and pursue goals with unwavering focus.

As the philosopher Blaise Pascal observed, *"Clarity of mind means clarity of passion, too; this is why a great and clear mind loves ardently and sees distinctly what it loves."* To cultivate clarity is to unlock not only clearer thinking but a deeper connection to purpose and meaning. It is the art of seeing the world — and ourselves — with unflinching honesty and unyielding hope.

Identifying Sources of Distortion

Clarity, while indispensable, is constantly under siege by forces both external and internal. These distortions do not merely cloud our perception; they actively shape how we experience the world. To see clearly, one must first recognize these sources of distortion. From societal pressures that subtly dictate norms to the personal insecurities that color our self-perception, each distortion chips away at the lens through which we view reality.

Societal Pressures: The Invisible Hand of Conformity

One of the most pervasive sources of distortion

is societal pressure, a force so subtle that its influence often goes unnoticed. From the moment we are born, society begins to mold our perceptions, embedding cultural norms, expectations, and values into the fabric of our identity. While these influences can foster community and shared purpose, they can also become a cage, limiting our ability to think and act independently.

The philosopher Jean-Jacques Rousseau observed this dynamic in his critique of social conformity, arguing that civilization often alienates individuals from their authentic selves. He described this phenomenon as a loss of "natural freedom," where individuals sacrifice clarity of thought in favor of acceptance within a group. In today's world, this manifests vividly in the digital age, where the curated perfection of social media creates unrealistic standards and fuels comparison.

Imagine the young artist who abandons their unique vision because it deviates from mainstream trends. Or consider the entrepreneur whose bold idea is diluted to fit into the familiar mold of what the market deems "acceptable."

In both cases, societal pressures distort the individual's clarity, steering decisions away from authenticity and toward conformity.

To combat this distortion, one must cultivate awareness of these pressures and develop the courage to question them. The ancient Greeks championed this practice through the Socratic method, which emphasized relentless questioning as a path to truth. By asking "Why?"—not once, but repeatedly—we can peel back the layers of societal conditioning and rediscover what truly resonates with our values.

Personal Insecurities: The Shadow Within

While societal pressures operate from the outside, personal insecurities work from within, casting long shadows over our ability to perceive clearly. Insecurities often stem from past experiences, where moments of failure or rejection leave lasting imprints. These emotional scars shape how we interpret the present, creating a feedback loop of doubt and fear.

Consider the example of impostor syndrome, a psychological pattern in which individuals doubt their accomplishments despite clear evidence of competence. This distortion convinces capable people that they are frauds, often causing them to shy away from opportunities or undervalue their contributions. The root of this insecurity lies in a distorted self-image—a lens that magnifies flaws while obscuring strengths.

Historical figures have wrestled with their insecurities, often finding that facing them head-on was the key to greatness. Abraham Lincoln, for instance, endured profound bouts of self-doubt and melancholy, which he referred to as his "melancholia." Yet, rather than allowing these insecurities to paralyze him, Lincoln channeled them into a deeper understanding of himself and the world. His ability to grapple with his inner turmoil became a source of resilience and empathy, enabling him to lead with extraordinary clarity during one of the most tumultuous periods in American history.

The path to overcoming insecurities begins with self-awareness. Practices such as mindfulness and journaling can help uncover the hidden fears that distort perception. By confronting these insecurities rather than avoiding them, we can begin to reclaim the clarity that lies on the other side of self-acceptance.

Misinformation: The Fog of Falsehoods

In an era defined by the rapid exchange of information, the proliferation of misinformation poses one of the greatest threats to clarity. From half-truths to outright lies, misinformation obscures reality, leading individuals and societies down paths built on faulty premises.

The 20th-century philosopher Hannah Arendt explored this phenomenon in her analysis of propaganda, noting that when lies are repeated often enough, they begin to resemble truth. This erosion of objective reality creates a fertile ground for manipulation, as seen in historical instances such as the rise of totalitarian regimes. Leaders who weaponized misinformation distorted public perception to such an extent that entire populations acted against their own interests, blinded by the illusion of clarity.

In today's context, the distortion of truth has become even more pervasive. Algorithms on social media platforms prioritize sensationalism over substance, creating echo chambers where misinformation thrives. This constant bombardment of half-truths and emotional appeals not only misleads but also fosters cynicism, leaving individuals unsure of what—or whom—to trust.

The antidote to misinformation lies in cultivating intellectual rigor and discernment. This means seeking out multiple perspectives, verifying sources, and embracing the humility to admit when we've been misled. As the Enlightenment thinker Voltaire famously quipped, *"Doubt is an uncomfortable condition, but certainty is a ridiculous one."* By embracing doubt as a tool for inquiry rather than a state of paralysis, we can navigate the fog of falsehoods and move closer to truth.

The Interplay of Distortions

These sources of distortion—societal pressures, personal insecurities, and misinformation—do not exist in isolation. They often intersect, amplifying their effects in complex and unpredictable ways. For example, a young professional may feel societal pressure to conform to a specific career path while simultaneously grappling with insecurities about their abilities. Add the influence of misleading narratives about "overnight success," and the result is a potent cocktail of distorted perception.

Recognizing this interplay is crucial for untangling the web of distortions. It requires a multi-faceted approach, one that addresses both internal and external factors. By questioning societal norms, confronting personal insecurities, and seeking truth amidst misinformation, we can begin to clear the lens through which we view the world.

Ultimately, clarity is not about achieving a distortion-free existence—a near-impossible task in a complex world—but about developing the resilience to navigate these distortions with awareness and intention. Like a sailor steering through turbulent seas, we must learn to adjust our course, guided by the unwavering pursuit of truth.

Tools for Clear Thinking

Clarity of thought is not an innate gift bestowed upon a select few; it is a skill, honed and sharpened through deliberate practice. Much like a craftsman relies on tools to shape raw materials into art, those seeking mental clarity must cultivate specific practices to refine their thinking. Mindfulness, critical thinking, and journaling stand out as three transformative tools for clearing the mental clutter that obscures perception. Together, they not only illuminate the path to clarity but also foster resilience and self-mastery in a chaotic world.

Mindfulness: The Anchor of Awareness

Mindfulness is the art of paying attention—not in haste, but with deliberate focus and without judgment. Rooted in ancient traditions, mindfulness has emerged as a powerful tool for modern clarity, offering a refuge from the distractions and distortions of daily life.

The origins of mindfulness can be traced back to Buddhist philosophy, where it was regarded as a cornerstone of enlightenment. The Buddha taught that mindfulness, or *sati*, involves cultivating an acute awareness of the present moment, allowing individuals to observe their thoughts and emotions as they arise. By developing this practice, one begins to see the mind's tendencies with greater clarity, disentangling truth from illusion.

In a contemporary context, mindfulness has been championed not only for its spiritual benefits but also for its practical applications. Studies in neuroscience reveal that mindfulness meditation rewires the brain, enhancing the prefrontal cortex—the seat of rational decision-making—while dampening the reactivity of the amygdala, which governs fear and impulsivity. This physiological shift equips individuals to navigate challenges with greater composure and insight.

Consider the story of Viktor Frankl, a Holocaust survivor and psychiatrist whose experience in Nazi concentration camps tested the limits of human resilience. In his seminal work, *Man's Search for Meaning*, Frankl described a pivotal realization: between stimulus and response lies a space, and in that space lies the power to choose. This perspective, grounded in mindful awareness, enabled Frankl to find meaning amid suffering and to act with clarity despite unimaginable adversity.

For modern readers, mindfulness can be cultivated through practices as simple as focused breathing, mindful walking, or setting aside moments of intentional stillness. Each act of mindfulness becomes a stepping stone toward greater clarity, helping to quiet the noise of external pressures and internal turbulence.

Critical Thinking: The Compass for Truth

While mindfulness anchors awareness, critical thinking sharpens discernment. It is the compass that guides us through the labyrinth of ideas, enabling us to differentiate between what is valid and what is misleading. In an age awash with information, the ability to think critically is not merely advantageous—it is essential.

Critical thinking begins with curiosity, a willingness to question assumptions and examine ideas from multiple angles. Socrates, the ancient Greek philosopher, exemplified this approach through his method of inquiry, which challenged students to articulate and defend their beliefs. By systematically questioning the validity of arguments, Socrates sought to uncover deeper truths, often exposing the fallacies hidden within seemingly self-evident ideas.

This same method holds relevance today, particularly in an era defined by rapid information exchange and polarized discourse. Critical thinking empowers individuals to assess evidence, identify biases, and construct well-reasoned conclusions. It transforms the passive consumption of information into an active process of evaluation, ensuring that decisions are guided by clarity rather than manipulation.

For instance, when faced with conflicting news reports or divergent opinions, a critical thinker refrains from immediate judgment. Instead, they seek to understand the sources, contexts, and motivations underlying the information. This practice not only guards against misinformation but also fosters intellectual humility — the recognition that one's knowledge is always incomplete and subject to refinement.

To cultivate critical thinking, readers can adopt techniques such as Socratic questioning, logic exercises, and engaging with diverse perspectives. These practices, though intellectually demanding, pave the way for a deeper and more accurate understanding of the world.

Journaling: The Mirror of the Mind

If mindfulness is the anchor and critical thinking the compass, journaling is the mirror—a reflective practice that reveals the intricacies of the mind. Through the act of writing, thoughts are externalized, clarified, and transformed from abstract musings into tangible insights.

The power of journaling lies in its ability to create distance between the thinker and their thoughts. By committing ideas to paper, the writer gains a fresh perspective, often uncovering patterns and solutions that remain hidden in the whirlwind of unexamined cognition.

Consider the example of Leonardo da Vinci, whose journals are a testament to the profound clarity achieved through disciplined reflection. Da Vinci's notebooks, filled with sketches, observations, and questions, reveal a mind constantly engaged in exploration and refinement. His ability to synthesize art, science, and philosophy stemmed in part from his commitment to documenting and interrogating his ideas.

In a more modern vein, journaling has been embraced as a therapeutic tool, offering individuals a safe space to process emotions, articulate goals, and track personal growth. Techniques such as stream-of-consciousness writing, gratitude journaling, and goal-setting exercises enable writers to focus their thoughts and intentions with precision.

For those seeking clarity, journaling provides an invaluable tool for self-inquiry. A simple practice, such as ending each day by jotting down reflections or questions, can illuminate paths forward that were previously obscured.

The Art of Simplifying Complexity

Underlying these tools is a shared principle: the importance of simplifying complexity. In a world characterized by overwhelm, clarity often emerges not from adding more but from subtracting the unnecessary.

This philosophy is echoed in the words of Leonardo da Vinci: *"Simplicity is the ultimate sophistication."* Whether applied to decision-making, relationships, or problem-solving, the ability to distill complexity into its essential components is a hallmark of clear thinking.

One way to practice simplification is through the concept of "mental decluttering," akin to Marie Kondo's method for tidying physical spaces. By identifying and discarding mental habits, beliefs, or distractions that no longer serve a purpose, individuals create room for clarity and focus.

In practice, this might involve setting boundaries around digital consumption, prioritizing tasks with laser focus, or consciously letting go of grudges and regrets. Each act of simplification contributes to a clearer mind, enabling the tools of mindfulness, critical thinking, and journaling to operate with greater effectiveness.

Clarity is not a single destination but an ongoing journey. The tools outlined here — mindfulness, critical thinking, and journaling — serve as both companions and guides, equipping individuals to navigate life's complexities with confidence and grace. By integrating these practices into daily routines, readers embark on a path of intentional living, where clarity becomes not just a fleeting state but a way of being.

Applying Clarity to Everyday Life

Clarity, when cultivated, is not a lofty concept meant to reside in abstract thought; it is a profoundly practical tool that transforms the way we navigate life. Its value lies in its application—how it shapes the decisions we make, the relationships we nurture, and the emotional well-being we cultivate. By bringing clarity into the rhythm of daily life, we unlock the ability to act with purpose and authenticity even amidst uncertainty.

Clarity in Decision-Making

At its core, clarity enhances decision-making by eliminating the noise that often complicates our choices. When faced with a crossroads—be it a career move, a relationship challenge, or a financial dilemma—the absence of clarity can lead to paralysis, procrastination, or impulsive actions. Conversely, clarity offers a structured way to assess the situation, weigh the options, and make decisions aligned with our values and goals.

Consider the decision-making process of Dwight D. Eisenhower, the former U.S. president and World War II general, whose ability to navigate complex situations was legendary. Eisenhower famously developed a decision-making matrix that prioritized tasks based on their urgency and importance. This approach allowed him to focus on what truly mattered while delegating or eliminating distractions.

In everyday life, we can emulate this by asking fundamental questions: *What outcome do I truly desire? What factors are clouding my judgment? What steps align with my core values?* By stripping away superficial concerns and anchoring decisions to a clear purpose, we not only make better choices but also approach them with greater confidence.

Clarity in Relationships

Relationships—whether personal or professional—thrive on clarity. Misunderstandings, unspoken expectations, and unresolved conflicts often stem from a lack of clear communication and perspective. By approaching interactions with clarity, we foster trust, empathy, and mutual understanding.

Philosopher Martin Buber explored this idea in his concept of the *I-Thou* relationship, which emphasizes genuine connection over transactional interactions. Buber argued that true relationships are rooted in seeing the other person clearly—not as an extension of our desires or fears, but as a distinct individual with their own needs and experiences.

In practice, this means cultivating the clarity to listen without preconceptions, to articulate our thoughts with honesty, and to address misunderstandings directly. For instance, consider the difference between saying, "You never listen to me," and, "I feel unheard when we talk about this topic." The latter statement, grounded in clarity, opens the door to resolution rather than defensiveness.

Clarity also empowers us to set healthy boundaries in relationships, ensuring that our interactions are rooted in mutual respect. By clearly identifying our own needs and articulating them without fear or guilt, we create space for relationships that are both supportive and authentic.

Clarity in Emotional Well-Being

Emotional clarity—the ability to understand and process one's feelings—is a cornerstone of mental health. In the absence of clarity, emotions can feel overwhelming, like a storm that clouds judgment and disrupts balance. But when approached with clarity, even the most intense emotions become manageable, offering insights rather than obstacles.

Take the ancient practice of Stoicism, which teaches that emotions themselves are not inherently problematic—it is our unexamined reactions to them that create suffering. Marcus Aurelius, a Roman emperor and Stoic philosopher, captured this wisdom in his *Meditations*, writing, *"You have power over your mind—not outside events. Realize this, and you will find strength."*

Applying this principle, we can use clarity to examine emotions with curiosity rather than resistance. For example, instead of succumbing to anger during a disagreement, we might pause and ask, *What triggered this feeling? Is it rooted in an unmet expectation, a fear, or a deeper frustration?* By identifying the underlying cause, we regain agency over our response, turning emotional turbulence into an opportunity for growth.

In daily life, cultivating emotional clarity might involve practices such as journaling about one's feelings, engaging in mindfulness exercises, or seeking support from trusted confidants. These habits create a foundation of emotional resilience, enabling us to navigate challenges with grace and composure.

Practical Examples of Clarity in Action

The true measure of clarity lies in its ability to impact real-life scenarios. Imagine a professional grappling with burnout. At first glance, the problem may seem insurmountable, driven by an overwhelming workload and external pressures. But with clarity, the individual can deconstruct the situation: *What specific factors are causing stress? Are there tasks that can be delegated or eliminated? What long-term adjustments would align work with personal values?* Armed with these insights, the professional can take targeted actions to regain balance and purpose.

Similarly, consider a parent struggling to connect with their teenage child. Without clarity, the relationship might be marred by frustration and miscommunication. But by approaching the situation with an open and curious perspective—seeking to understand the child's experiences and expressing their own feelings with honesty—the parent creates a foundation for deeper connection.

Even mundane decisions benefit from clarity. For instance, planning a weekly grocery trip might seem trivial, but without clarity, it can devolve into a stressful ordeal of forgotten items and wasted time. By approaching the task with intentionality—creating a clear list based on needs and preferences—the process becomes efficient and stress-free.

Building a Daily Practice of Clarity

Applying clarity to everyday life is not a one-time endeavor; it is a habit, cultivated through consistent effort. Small, intentional actions compound over time, transforming the way we approach decisions, relationships, and emotions.

One practical strategy is the "pause and reflect" technique: before reacting to a situation, take a moment to pause, breathe, and ask, *What is truly happening here?* This brief interlude allows us to respond with intention rather than impulse, ensuring that our actions align with our values.

Another approach is to schedule regular periods of reflection, such as a weekly review. During this time, evaluate the past week's decisions, interactions, and emotions, asking questions like, *What went well? What could have been handled differently? What lessons can I carry forward?*

Ultimately, clarity becomes a lens through which we view the world—not as an occasional tool but as a way of being. It empowers us to live with purpose, act with conviction, and connect with others in meaningful ways. In doing so, we find that even in the chaos of life, clarity offers a sense of calm, direction, and fulfillment.

CHAPTER 2: BREAKING ILLUSIONS – CHALLENGING YOUR ASSUMPTIONS

The Nature of Assumptions

Assumptions are the silent architects of perception. They shape how we interpret events, understand others, and navigate the world. Often, these underlying beliefs operate unnoticed, steering our thoughts and actions without conscious input. Yet, when left unchecked, assumptions can distort reality, breeding misunderstandings, missed opportunities, and flawed decisions.

To understand the power of assumptions, we must first recognize their origin. Assumptions are mental shortcuts, born from the brain's need to simplify complexity. They allow us to make sense of the world quickly by filling gaps in our knowledge with educated guesses. While this process is essential for efficiency—imagine having to relearn basic truths every day—it also carries risks. When assumptions go unexamined, they become rigid frameworks that resist new information, trapping us in cycles of misunderstanding and error.

Assumptions as Distortions of Reality

One of the clearest examples of how assumptions distort reality can be found in the realm of human interaction. Consider a scenario where a friend fails to respond to a message. Without clarity, the mind begins to craft explanations: *They must be upset with me*, or *They're ignoring me on purpose*. These interpretations, driven by assumption rather than evidence, shape emotions and behavior—often leading to unnecessary conflict or anxiety.

Now magnify this dynamic onto a larger scale. Throughout history, assumptions have influenced pivotal decisions, sometimes with catastrophic consequences. A stark example is the Charge of the Light Brigade during the Crimean War. Miscommunication and assumptions about orders led British cavalrymen into a disastrous frontal assault against heavily armed Russian forces. The event, immortalized in Alfred Lord Tennyson's poem, serves as a grim reminder of how unchecked assumptions can lead to dire outcomes.

In everyday life, the impact of assumptions is less dramatic but no less significant. They guide how we interpret body language, tone, and intent—often projecting our insecurities or biases onto others. Without realizing it, we paint over the canvas of reality with the brushstrokes of our own preconceived notions, obscuring the true picture.

Historical Lessons in Assumption

The dangers of assumptions are not limited to interpersonal misunderstandings; they extend to entire societies and historical movements. One profound example comes from the trial of Galileo Galilei in the 17th century. At the time, the assumption that Earth was the center of the universe had been entrenched for centuries. This geocentric view, supported by religious doctrine and cultural tradition, shaped not only scientific inquiry but also societal values.

When Galileo presented evidence supporting the heliocentric model—proposing that the Earth revolved around the sun—he was met with fierce resistance. His findings challenged the core assumptions of his era, threatening the established order. Galileo's trial and subsequent condemnation by the Catholic Church illustrate how deeply rooted assumptions can hinder progress and obscure truth.

These historical lessons resonate today, reminding us that assumptions often reflect the limitations of our current understanding rather
than absolute truths. By acknowledging this,
we open the door to curiosity and discovery,
replacing rigid certainty with a willingness to
question.

How Assumptions Shape Identity

Assumptions are not just external projections;
they also influence how we perceive ourselves.
These self-assumptions—beliefs about our abilities, worth, and potential—can be both empowering and limiting. For example, a person
who assumes they are inherently bad at public
speaking may avoid opportunities to practice,
reinforcing the belief and missing chances for
growth.

Psychologist Carol Dweck's research on fixed
versus growth mindsets sheds light on this phenomenon. Individuals with a fixed mindset assume their traits and abilities are static, leading
to avoidance of challenges and fear of failure. In

contrast, those with a growth mindset assume that abilities can be developed through effort and learning, fostering resilience and adaptability.

This shift in assumptions has profound implications for personal development. By challenging self-limiting beliefs and adopting a more dynamic view of potential, we create space for transformation. As philosopher Ralph Waldo Emerson observed, *"The mind, once stretched by a new idea, never returns to its original dimensions."*

The Path to Challenging Assumptions

Recognizing the role of assumptions is the first step toward clarity, but it is not enough to simply acknowledge them. Challenging assumptions requires deliberate effort, intellectual humility, and a commitment to seeking truth.

One powerful approach is to adopt a mindset of inquiry. Instead of accepting assumptions at face value, ask questions that probe their validity:

- *What evidence supports this belief?*

- Are there alternative explanations?

- What might I be overlooking?

The practice of inquiry mirrors the scientific method, where hypotheses are tested and refined rather than accepted uncritically. This approach not only exposes flaws in assumptions but also cultivates a habit of open-mindedness, allowing for continuous learning and growth.

Another strategy is to seek diverse perspectives. When we engage with individuals from different backgrounds, cultures, or disciplines, we are exposed to viewpoints that challenge our assumptions. This exchange fosters empathy and broadens our understanding, revealing nuances that might otherwise go unnoticed.

Consider the philosopher Søren Kierkegaard's assertion that *"Life can only be understood backwards; but it must be lived forwards."* This paradox highlights the need for reflection and reassessment, as assumptions often become clearer in hindsight. By revisiting past experiences with a critical eye, we can uncover the assumptions that shaped our actions and refine our approach moving forward.

The Freedom of Clarity

Breaking free from the grip of assumptions is not an easy task, but it is a liberating one. As assumptions are challenged and discarded, the mind becomes more agile, more curious, and more aligned with reality. This freedom extends beyond intellectual clarity; it transforms how we engage with the world, fostering deeper connections, better decisions, and a profound sense of purpose.

The philosopher Jiddu Krishnamurti once said, *"The ability to observe without evaluating is the highest form of intelligence."* This observation captures the essence of clarity: the ability to see without distortion, to understand without assumption. By cultivating this quality, we unlock the potential to navigate life with greater wisdom and authenticity, unburdened by the illusions that once clouded our vision.

Spotting Cognitive Biases

Cognitive biases are the mind's shortcuts—unconscious patterns of thought that simplify decision-making but often distort reality. While these biases help us navigate the complexities of daily life with efficiency, they can also lead us astray, obscuring clarity and reinforcing false assumptions. Recognizing and overcoming cognitive biases is not merely an intellectual exercise; it is a fundamental step toward living with greater purpose and insight.

To understand the nature of biases, we must first acknowledge their origin. The human brain, designed for survival rather than precision, developed these mental shortcuts as adaptive tools. In ancient times, when decisions often carried life-or-death stakes, swift judgments could mean the difference between safety and peril. However, in the modern world, where nuance and complexity reign, these biases can cloud our thinking, creating blind spots that hinder progress and understanding.

Confirmation Bias: Seeking What We Want to See

Among the most pervasive cognitive biases is

confirmation bias—the tendency to seek, interpret, and remember information that aligns with our preexisting beliefs. Confirmation bias operates subtly, reinforcing assumptions and narrowing perspective. Rather than viewing evidence objectively, the mind gravitates toward data that validates its current worldview, discarding anything that contradicts it.

Consider the story of Ignaz Semmelweis, a 19th-century Hungarian physician whose discovery of handwashing as a means to prevent infection was met with widespread skepticism. Despite clear evidence that handwashing reduced mortality rates in maternity wards, many of Semmelweis's contemporaries dismissed his findings. Why? Their preconceived notions about the causes of illness—rooted in the "miasma" theory of bad air—blinded them to the truth. Their confirmation bias prevented them from considering a paradigm-shifting idea, delaying the adoption of a lifesaving practice.

In today's polarized world, confirmation bias manifests in how individuals consume information. Social media algorithms, designed to maximize engagement, often exacerbate this bias by presenting users with content that reinforces their existing views. This creates echo chambers where opposing perspectives are rarely encountered, further entrenching beliefs.

Overcoming confirmation bias begins with cultivating intellectual humility — the willingness to acknowledge that one's knowledge is incomplete and subject to change. Asking questions such as, *What evidence might challenge my belief?* or *Am I seeking information to learn, or merely to validate?* can help disrupt this pattern.

Anchoring Bias: The Power of First Impressions

Another cognitive trap is anchoring bias, where the mind fixates on the first piece of information encountered, using it as a reference point for subsequent judgments. This bias is particularly insidious because it can occur without conscious awareness, subtly influencing decisions in ways that feel rational but are anything but.

For instance, when negotiating the price of a car, the seller's initial offer often serves as an anchor, shaping the buyer's perception of what constitutes a "reasonable" counteroffer. Even when the anchor is arbitrary, its influence lingers, skewing judgment.

The effects of anchoring extend beyond negotiations. In courtroom settings, research has shown that judges' sentencing decisions can be influenced by irrelevant numerical anchors, such as the suggested penalties from prosecuting attorneys. This highlights the pervasive nature of anchoring and its ability to distort even critical, high-stakes decisions.

To counteract anchoring bias, one must learn to step back and reassess situations independently of initial reference points. Practicing deliberate skepticism—asking, *Why am I accepting this starting point as valid?*—can help neutralize the anchor's influence.

Availability Bias: The Ease of Recall

Availability bias occurs when the mind overestimates the likelihood of events based on how easily they can be recalled. This bias explains why people often fear plane crashes more than car accidents, despite the latter being far more common. Dramatic, vivid events stick in memory, shaping perceptions in ways that are disproportionate to their actual frequency.

In personal and professional contexts, availability bias can lead to flawed risk assessments. For example, a business leader who recently witnessed a competitor's failure may become overly cautious, assuming similar risks loom closer than they do. Conversely, positive but atypical outcomes—such as a "unicorn" startup achieving massive success—may inflate optimism, leading to unrealistic expectations.

Overcoming availability bias requires cultivating an awareness of how memory and emotion influence judgment. Seeking out data and objective metrics can provide a counterbalance to subjective recall, grounding decisions in reality rather than perception.

Techniques for Recognizing and Disrupting Biases

While each bias operates uniquely, their effects share a common theme: they distort clarity by narrowing the mind's focus. The key to mitigating their influence lies in deliberate self-reflection and the adoption of strategies that foster objectivity.

One effective technique is perspective-taking — the practice of imagining how others might view the same situation. By stepping into another's shoes, we challenge our own assumptions and biases, expanding our understanding. This approach aligns with the wisdom of ancient philosophers like Epictetus, who taught that clarity emerges when we learn to see beyond our limited vantage point.

Another powerful tool is the habit of slowing down decision-making. Cognitive biases often thrive in fast-paced, reactive environments where there is little time for reflection. Pausing to evaluate the validity of one's assumptions, seeking out diverse opinions, and weighing alternative explanations can disrupt the automatic patterns that biases reinforce.

Finally, cultivating a mindset of lifelong learning can inoculate against the rigidity that biases create. By embracing curiosity and treating beliefs as hypotheses to be tested rather than truths to be defended, we create space for growth and discovery.

The Liberating Power of Awareness

Recognizing and addressing cognitive biases is not about achieving perfect objectivity — a near-impossible goal for any human mind. Instead, it is about developing the awareness and tools to navigate biases with greater intention. The philosopher and mathematician Alfred North Whitehead once wrote, *"It requires a very unusual mind to undertake the analysis of the obvious."* Spotting cognitive biases requires just such a willingness to question what feels self-evident, peeling back layers of thought to uncover deeper truths.

As we cultivate this skill, we not only refine our decision-making but also strengthen our capacity for empathy, understanding, and connection. In a world often divided by misunderstanding, the ability to see clearly — unclouded by bias — is a profound act of wisdom.

Challenging Long-Held Beliefs

Beliefs are the architecture of our inner world. They form the foundation upon which we build our identities, interpret experiences, and navigate the complexities of life. Yet, the very beliefs that provide stability can also become barriers to growth when they remain unexamined. Questioning long-held beliefs is among the most uncomfortable—and transformative—acts a person can undertake. It is an act of courage that invites uncertainty but promises clarity, renewal, and profound personal evolution.

The Discomfort of Questioning

Why do we resist questioning our beliefs? The answer lies in the psychological comfort they provide. Beliefs offer a sense of order in an unpredictable world. They anchor our identity, shape our decisions, and help us interpret events in ways that feel consistent and coherent. To challenge them is to confront uncertainty, a state that the human mind instinctively seeks to avoid.

The German philosopher Friedrich Nietzsche captured this tension when he wrote, *"A casual stroll through the lunatic asylum shows that faith does not prove anything."* Nietzsche wasn't dismissing faith outright but highlighting its potential to obscure truth when accepted without scrutiny. Long-held beliefs can become prisons of certainty, trapping us in perspectives that no longer serve us.

Consider the example of Galileo Galilei, whose advocacy for the heliocentric model defied the deeply entrenched geocentric worldview of his time. For centuries, the belief that Earth was the center of the universe had shaped not only scientific thought but also religious doctrine and cultural identity. Questioning this belief was seen as heretical, yet Galileo's persistence in seeking the truth reshaped humanity's understanding of the cosmos. His journey illustrates the transformative power—and the profound discomfort—of challenging prevailing beliefs.

The Transformative Growth That Follows

While questioning beliefs is inherently uncomfortable, it is also profoundly liberating. When we examine our assumptions and let go of outdated ideas, we create space for new perspectives, deeper understanding, and personal growth.

Take, for instance, the story of Nelson Mandela. Imprisoned for 27 years under South Africa's apartheid regime, Mandela had every reason to harbor hatred and resentment toward his oppressors. Yet, during his time in prison, he challenged the beliefs he had once held about vengeance and justice. Instead of seeking retribution, Mandela embraced reconciliation, a radical shift in perspective that not only transformed his personal outlook but also became the cornerstone of South Africa's peaceful transition to democracy.

Mandela's example underscores the power of reexamining beliefs. By questioning the narratives that shape our understanding of justice, forgiveness, and humanity, he transcended the limitations of his circumstances and inspired a nation to do the same.

Steps to Reevaluate and Revise Beliefs

Revising long-held beliefs is not a passive process; it requires intentional effort and a willingness to embrace uncertainty. The following steps offer a framework for navigating this transformative journey:

1. **Identify Core Beliefs**: Begin by examining the beliefs that shape your identity, values, and decisions. These might include assumptions about success, relationships, morality, or your own abilities. Reflect on their origins: *Where did this belief come from? Is it rooted in personal experience, cultural norms, or inherited values?*

2. **Examine Contradictory Evidence**: Actively seek out information or perspectives that challenge your existing beliefs. This process, while uncomfortable, helps illuminate blind spots and exposes the limitations of one-sided thinking. For example, if you believe that success requires relentless sacrifice, explore stories of individuals who achieved fulfillment through balance and self-care.

3. **Engage in Open Dialogue**: Conversations with individuals who hold different beliefs can be powerful catalysts for growth. Approach these dialogues with curiosity rather than defensiveness, asking questions such as, *What experiences have shaped your perspective?* and *How do*

you interpret this issue differently than I do?

4. **Experiment with New Perspectives**: Testing alternative beliefs in real-life scenarios can provide valuable insights. If you've long believed that taking risks leads to failure, experiment with a small, calculated risk and observe the outcome. These experiences often reveal the limitations of entrenched beliefs while fostering confidence in alternative approaches.

5. **Practice Self-Compassion**: Letting go of long-held beliefs can feel like losing a part of yourself. It's important to approach this process with self-compassion, recognizing that growth often involves discomfort. Remind yourself that revising beliefs is not a sign of weakness but a testament to your willingness to evolve.

The Ripple Effect of Questioning Beliefs

When we challenge our beliefs, the impact extends far beyond ourselves. As we become more open-minded and adaptable, we inspire those around us to do the same. This ripple effect is evident in the stories of individuals and movements that have reshaped history by daring to question the status quo.

Consider the civil rights movement in the United States. Leaders like Martin Luther King Jr. and Rosa Parks challenged deeply ingrained societal beliefs about race, equality, and justice. Their courage not only catalyzed systemic change but also invited millions to reevaluate their own assumptions about prejudice and privilege.

On a smaller scale, questioning beliefs within families or communities can lead to more authentic connections and shared understanding. When individuals are willing to discuss and reconsider differing perspectives, they create an environment of trust and mutual growth.

The Unfolding Journey

The process of questioning and revising beliefs is not a one-time event but an ongoing journey. As the world changes and we encounter new experiences, our beliefs must adapt to remain relevant and true. Philosopher John Dewey captured this dynamic when he wrote, *"Growth itself is the only moral end."* To grow, we must be willing to let go of certainty and embrace the unknown.

By challenging long-held beliefs, we break free from the limitations of outdated perspectives and unlock the potential for greater clarity, purpose, and connection. This act, though daunting, is among the most empowering steps we can take toward living an authentic and fulfilling life.

Building Mental Flexibility

The ability to adapt is one of the greatest markers of resilience and clarity. Mental flexibility is the skill that allows individuals to pivot gracefully in the face of change, uncertainty, or contradiction. It is the antidote to rigidity and the foundation of a dynamic, growth-oriented perspective. In a world that is constantly evolving, mental flexibility is not just an advantage; it is a necessity.

The Nature of Mental Flexibility

Mental flexibility involves holding multiple perspectives simultaneously, shifting viewpoints as new information emerges, and approaching challenges with creativity and openness. Unlike mental rigidity, which clings to fixed ideas and fears uncertainty, mental flexibility thrives in ambiguity. It acknowledges that life's complexities cannot always be solved with simple answers and invites a spirit of curiosity and exploration.

The Stoic philosopher Epictetus embodied this principle when he advised, *"Make the best use of what is in your power, and take the rest as it happens."* This mindset reflects a profound understanding of adaptability: focusing on what can be controlled while remaining open to the unpredictable. Mental flexibility does not mean abandoning values or principles; rather, it involves responding thoughtfully to circumstances without being tethered to preconceived notions.

The Role of Uncertainty in Growth

Uncertainty is often viewed as a source of anxiety, yet it is also a catalyst for growth. When we step into the unknown, we encounter opportunities to expand our understanding, develop new skills, and challenge assumptions. The philosopher Søren Kierkegaard referred to this as the "dizziness of freedom," the disorienting yet exhilarating experience of confronting endless possibilities.

Consider the scientific process as a model of mental flexibility. Researchers begin with a hypothesis but remain open to the possibility that their assumptions might be wrong. When experiments yield unexpected results, it is not a failure but an opportunity to refine theories and uncover new truths. This iterative process mirrors the practice of mental flexibility in everyday life, where mistakes and surprises become stepping stones rather than stumbling blocks.

Historical figures who embraced uncertainty often achieved transformative breakthroughs. Albert Einstein, for instance, revolutionized physics by questioning long-held assumptions about space and time. His willingness to entertain radical ideas, coupled with rigorous inquiry, exemplifies the interplay between mental flexibility and intellectual achievement.

Cultivating an Adaptive Mindset

Developing mental flexibility is not an innate talent but a skill that can be cultivated through deliberate practice. At its core, it requires a willingness to embrace discomfort and let go of the need for absolute certainty.

One key practice is reframing challenges as opportunities. When faced with a setback, ask, *What can I learn from this? How might this experience lead to growth?* By shifting focus from the obstacle itself to the potential it holds, you foster a mindset of adaptability.

Another powerful tool is exposure to diverse perspectives. Engaging with people, cultures, and ideas that differ from your own broadens understanding and encourages creative problem-solving. This practice aligns with the philosophy of the Enlightenment thinker John Stuart Mill, who argued that exposure to opposing viewpoints sharpens one's own beliefs and fosters intellectual humility.

Mindfulness also plays a vital role in cultivating mental flexibility. By observing thoughts and emotions without judgment, mindfulness creates space to respond intentionally rather than react impulsively. This pause allows for a more measured and adaptable approach to challenges.

The Benefits of Mental Flexibility

The rewards of mental flexibility extend far beyond intellectual clarity. On a personal level, it fosters resilience, enabling individuals to navigate adversity with grace. When plans unravel or circumstances shift unexpectedly, mental flexibility helps maintain a sense of equilibrium, turning setbacks into stepping stones.

In relationships, mental flexibility enhances empathy and communication. By considering others' perspectives and adapting to their needs, we strengthen connections and build mutual trust. For example, a leader who listens to their team's input and adjusts strategies accordingly fosters a collaborative environment where innovation can thrive.

At a societal level, mental flexibility is essential for addressing complex challenges such as climate change, inequality, and technological disruption. These issues require solutions that transcend traditional frameworks, demanding the kind of adaptive thinking that mental flexibility provides.

One striking example is the Apollo 13 mission, where NASA engineers and astronauts faced a life-threatening crisis when an oxygen tank exploded mid-flight. The team's ability to think creatively under pressure—improvising a carbon dioxide filter with limited resources—exemplified the power of adaptability in overcoming seemingly insurmountable challenges.

The Philosophical Foundations of Adaptability

Philosophical traditions across cultures have long emphasized the importance of adaptability. In Taoism, the concept of *wu wei*—often translated as "effortless action"—encourages aligning with the natural flow of life rather than resisting it. This principle teaches that flexibility, rather than force, leads to harmony and success.

Similarly, the Zen Buddhist practice of *shoshin*, or "beginner's mind," emphasizes approaching each moment with openness and curiosity. By letting go of preconceived notions, practitioners cultivate a mindset that is receptive to new possibilities and insights.

These philosophies remind us that adaptability is not about passivity but about being attuned to the present moment and responding with intention. They invite us to embrace life's uncertainties with a spirit of exploration, finding strength in the very fluidity that challenges us.

Practical Steps for Developing Mental Flexibility

To build mental flexibility, consider incorporating the following practices into your daily life:

- **Embrace the Unknown**: Challenge yourself to step outside your comfort zone regularly, whether by trying a new activity, engaging with unfamiliar ideas, or taking calculated risks.

- **Reflect on Setbacks**: When facing a challenge, take time to reflect on what it taught you and how it might shape your future approach.

- **Practice Curiosity**: Approach problems and interactions with a mindset of curiosity rather than judgment. Ask open-ended questions to uncover new perspectives.

- **Stay Present**: Use mindfulness techniques to anchor yourself in the present, reducing reactivity and enhancing clarity.

The Power of Mental Agility

Mental flexibility is not about abandoning principles or surrendering to chaos; it is about cultivating a mindset that thrives in complexity. By embracing uncertainty, adapting to change, and remaining open to growth, we unlock the ability to navigate life with clarity, resilience, and purpose.

As the Greek philosopher Heraclitus observed, *"The only constant in life is change."* By building mental flexibility, we align ourselves with this truth, transforming life's uncertainties into opportunities for discovery and transformation.

CHAPTER 3: THE POWER OF CONTEXT – UNDERSTANDING THE BIGGER PICTURE

The Role of Context in Shaping Perspective

Perspective is not formed in a vacuum. It is sculpted by the interplay of circumstances, experiences, and environments that surround us. Context is the unseen frame within which we interpret the world, shaping not only what we see but how we see it. To understand the power of context is to unlock a deeper appreciation of how our decisions, judgments, and relationships are influenced by forces that often go unnoticed.

Context as a Lens

Imagine looking at a painting. Without knowledge of its history, the artist's intent, or the cultural moment that inspired it, your interpretation may be limited or even misguided. The same principle applies to life. Context serves as the lens through which we assign meaning to events, making it indispensable for accurate understanding.

Take, for instance, the historical event of the Cuban Missile Crisis in 1962. For many, it is remembered as a dramatic standoff between the

United States and the Soviet Union—a moment when nuclear war seemed imminent. Yet, the full significance of the crisis emerges only when viewed in the broader context of the Cold War. The decades of ideological rivalry, the arms race, and the fear of mutual destruction created a backdrop that shaped the decisions of both nations. Without this context, the crisis might appear as an isolated act of aggression rather than a complex episode of strategic brinkmanship.

This example underscores how context enriches understanding. It illuminates the motivations, constraints, and stakes involved, transforming a simplistic narrative into a nuanced story.

The Perils of Context Blindness

When context is ignored, misunderstandings and poor decisions often follow. One of the most striking examples comes from the infamous Salem witch trials of the late 17th century. A wave of accusations led to the execution of twenty people, driven by fear and hysteria. At first glance, the trials seem like a tragic anomaly, a bizarre eruption of paranoia.

However, when viewed in context, a more complex picture emerges. The Salem community was grappling with social tensions, economic hardships, and the lingering trauma of frontier warfare. These factors created a fertile ground for scapegoating, amplifying the hysteria. By neglecting the broader context, the community misinterpreted their struggles, attributing them to malevolent forces rather than systemic issues.

This lesson resonates today, reminding us that context is not merely a backdrop; it is a critical component of interpretation. Without it, we risk making judgments that are not only inaccurate but also harmful.

Context in Personal Decision-Making

Context also plays a pivotal role in personal decisions. Consider the story of Malala Yousafzai, the Nobel Peace Prize laureate who became an advocate for girls' education after surviving a Taliban attack. Malala's perspective on education was profoundly shaped by the context of her upbringing in Pakistan's Swat Valley, where access to education for girls was restricted.

What makes Malala's story remarkable is her ability to recognize the broader context of her circumstances. Rather than accepting her situation as inevitable, she understood it as a reflection of systemic inequality and cultural norms. This awareness empowered her to challenge those norms, turning her personal struggle into a global movement.

For individuals, the lesson is clear: understanding the context of your circumstances can provide clarity and direction. By asking questions like, *What external factors are shaping my situation? How do historical or cultural forces influence my choices?*, you gain a deeper insight into the forces at play, enabling more informed and purposeful decisions.

The Interplay of Context and Empathy

Context is not only vital for understanding events; it is also essential for fostering empathy. When we consider the context of another person's actions, we are better equipped to see their perspective and respond with compassion.

The story of Japanese-American internment during World War II offers a poignant example. In the wake of the Pearl Harbor attack, over 120,000 Japanese Americans were forcibly relocated to internment camps, driven by a context of fear and wartime prejudice. For decades, this episode was justified as a necessary security measure. However, as historical context was revisited, the policy was revealed to be a gross injustice rooted in racism and paranoia.

By understanding the broader context, we not only recognize the mistakes of the past but also develop a deeper empathy for those who suffered. Context humanizes individuals, transforming abstract judgments into meaningful connections.

Context in Modern Challenges

In today's interconnected world, context is more critical than ever. Global challenges such as climate change, economic inequality, and social polarization cannot be understood—or addressed—without a contextual lens.

Consider climate change. At a glance, it may

seem like a purely environmental issue. Yet, when placed in context, it becomes clear that it is also a social, economic, and political challenge. The industrial practices of developed nations, the vulnerabilities of low-income communities, and the interplay of global governance all contribute to the problem. Understanding this context is essential for crafting effective solutions that address not only the symptoms but also the root causes.

Similarly, in the workplace, leaders who fail to consider context often make decisions that backfire. A new policy may seem logical on paper but falter when implemented because it fails to account for the unique culture, values, or challenges of the organization. Recognizing and respecting these contextual factors is key to effective leadership.

Practical Applications of Contextual Thinking

To harness the power of context, individuals can adopt practices that deepen their awareness and broaden their perspective. One approach is to cultivate curiosity—asking questions about the "why" and "how" behind events rather than accepting them at face value. For example, instead of reacting emotionally to a colleague's abrupt comment, consider the potential context: Are they under stress? Is there a misunderstanding that needs clarification?

Another strategy is to seek diverse viewpoints. Engaging with people from different backgrounds, disciplines, or cultures expands your understanding of the factors shaping a situation. This practice aligns with the wisdom of the Renaissance polymath Leonardo da Vinci, who believed that multiple perspectives were essential for creativity and insight.

Finally, reflection is a powerful tool for contextual thinking. By regularly reviewing decisions and experiences, asking questions like, *What broader factors influenced this situation? What lessons can I draw from this context?*, you develop a habit of mindful awareness that enhances clarity and decision-making.

The Bigger Picture

Context transforms fragments into a cohesive whole. It reveals the intricate connections between people, events, and environments, enabling us to see beyond surface-level interpretations. By embracing the power of context, we move closer to understanding the bigger picture — a perspective that not only clarifies the present but also illuminates the path forward.

Expanding Your Viewpoint

Perspective is both a gift and a limitation. While it allows us to make sense of the world through our unique lens, it also constrains us, tethering our understanding to the boundaries of our experience. Expanding your viewpoint is the antidote to this constraint. It is an act of intellectual and emotional openness, a willingness to step beyond the familiar and explore the broader forces that shape reality.

The Value of Historical Parallels

History, as the philosopher George Santayana famously warned, is often repeated by those who fail to learn from it. Yet, when we view history through the lens of context, it offers a treasure trove of insights that can broaden our understanding of contemporary challenges.

Examining historical parallels allows us to see patterns, consequences, and potential solutions with greater clarity.

Take, for instance, the Great Depression of the 1930s and the global financial crisis of 2008. At first glance, these events appear distinct, separated by decades and shaped by different economic landscapes. Yet, a closer examination reveals striking similarities: both were fueled by speculative bubbles, inadequate regulatory frameworks, and widespread public panic. By understanding these parallels, policymakers and economists in 2008 were able to draw lessons from the past, implementing measures like bank bailouts and stimulus packages to prevent a more catastrophic collapse.

For individuals, the same principle applies. Consider a personal conflict that seems insurmountable. By reflecting on similar situations you've faced—or by studying how others have navigated comparable challenges—you gain a broader perspective, uncovering patterns and potential pathways forward. History, whether personal or collective, becomes a guide for making informed and thoughtful decisions.

The Power of Diverse Opinions

If history broadens our temporal perspective, diverse opinions expand our conceptual horizon. Engaging with viewpoints that differ from our own is one of the most effective ways to challenge assumptions, refine understanding, and cultivate empathy.

The Renaissance polymath Leonardo da Vinci exemplified this principle. Renowned for his ability to merge art, science, and philosophy, da Vinci sought inspiration from a wide range of disciplines and perspectives. His studies spanned anatomy, engineering, and astronomy, each informing the other and enriching his creative vision. This interdisciplinary curiosity enabled da Vinci to produce works of genius, from the *Mona Lisa* to designs for flying machines.

In today's world, the practice of seeking diverse opinions is equally vital. When we confine ourselves to echo chambers—whether in social media, professional settings, or personal relationships—we reinforce existing biases and miss opportunities for growth. By stepping into spaces where our views are challenged, we expand our capacity to think critically and creatively.

For example, consider a business leader navigating a challenging market. By consulting stakeholders from various departments, including those with differing priorities and expertise, the leader gains a more comprehensive understanding of the situation. This approach not only leads to better decisions but also fosters collaboration and trust.

Analyzing Systemic Factors

Expanding your viewpoint also involves recognizing the systemic forces at play in any given situation. While individual actions and decisions are important, they are often shaped by broader structures—economic, social, cultural, and political—that operate behind the scenes. Understanding these systems provides a deeper context for interpreting events and making informed choices.

Consider the civil rights movement in the United States. While the courage of individuals like

Rosa Parks and Martin Luther King Jr. played a pivotal role, their actions were embedded within a larger system of systemic racism and inequality. Recognizing this context allowed the movement to address not only individual injustices but also the structural barriers that perpetuated discrimination.

In personal and professional life, the same principle applies. Suppose a team at work is struggling to meet deadlines. A narrow perspective might focus solely on individual performance, attributing the issue to a lack of effort or skill. However, a systemic analysis might reveal deeper causes, such as unclear communication, inadequate resources, or unrealistic expectations. By addressing these systemic factors, the team can achieve sustainable improvement rather than merely treating symptoms.

Practical Strategies for Broadening Perspective

Broadening perspective is not a passive process; it requires intentionality and effort. One effective strategy is to cultivate curiosity. When faced with a challenge, ask questions like, *What am I missing? What other factors might be influencing this situation?* This mindset invites exploration and prevents premature conclusions.

Another approach is to seek out interdisciplinary learning. By studying fields outside your immediate expertise, you gain new tools and frameworks for understanding the world. For instance, an artist who studies psychology might develop a deeper appreciation for human behavior, enriching their creative work. Similarly, a scientist who explores philosophy might gain insights into the ethical implications of their research.

Travel is another powerful way to expand perspective. Experiencing different cultures and ways of life challenges preconceived notions and fosters a more global outlook. As Mark Twain observed, *"Travel is fatal to prejudice, bigotry, and narrow-mindedness."* By stepping outside your comfort zone, you open yourself to the richness and diversity of human experience.

Finally, reflection plays a crucial role in broadening perspective. Take time to revisit past decisions, asking, *What influenced my thinking at the time? How might I view this situation dif-*

ferently now? This practice not only deepens self-awareness but also builds the habit of contextual thinking.

The Transformative Power of Perspective

Expanding your viewpoint is more than an intellectual exercise; it is a transformative practice that reshapes how you engage with the world. When you embrace the broader context, seek diverse opinions, and analyze systemic factors, you cultivate a mindset that is both curious and compassionate. This mindset equips you to navigate complexity with clarity, respond to challenges with creativity, and connect with others on a deeper level.

In a world that often feels fragmented and polarized, the ability to expand your perspective is a powerful antidote. It bridges divides, fosters understanding, and reveals the interconnectedness of all things. As the philosopher Marcus Aurelius wrote, *"The universe is change; our life is what our thoughts make it."* By broadening our thoughts, we create a life—and a world—of greater clarity, purpose, and possibility.

Avoiding Tunnel Vision

Tunnel vision, while often unintentional, is one of the greatest threats to clear thinking. It occurs when we fixate on a single idea, solution, or perspective, excluding alternatives and losing sight of the bigger picture. Though this narrow focus can sometimes provide clarity in specific situations, it often leads to missed opportunities, flawed decisions, and unnecessary conflict. Recognizing and avoiding tunnel vision is essential for navigating life's complexities with wisdom and flexibility.

The Dangers of Narrow Thinking

The most immediate danger of tunnel vision is its ability to distort judgment. When we lock onto a particular viewpoint, we filter out information that contradicts it, reinforcing our bias and limiting our understanding. This narrowing of perspective can create a false sense of certainty, blinding us to nuance and preventing us from adapting when circumstances change.

History is replete with examples of how tunnel vision has led to disastrous consequences. One of the most striking is the failure of France's Maginot Line during World War II. In the years following World War I, France constructed an elaborate system of fortifications along its eastern border, believing it would protect the country from a German invasion. However, this defensive strategy was based on the assumption that future conflicts would mirror the static trench warfare of the previous war.

When Germany invaded in 1940, it bypassed the Maginot Line entirely, advancing through Belgium and rendering the fortifications obsolete. The French military's tunnel vision—its inability to anticipate a different kind of warfare—contributed to one of the most devastating defeats in modern history.

On a smaller scale, tunnel vision can manifest in everyday decisions. Imagine a professional who is so fixated on achieving a promotion that they neglect opportunities for personal growth, relationship-building, or even career pivots that might offer greater fulfillment. By focusing narrowly on a single goal, they risk missing the richness and diversity of possibilities around them.

The Psychological Roots of Tunnel Vision

Tunnel vision often arises from deeply ingrained psychological tendencies. One such tendency is the brain's preference for simplicity. Faced with complex problems, the mind gravitates toward straightforward solutions, even when those solutions are incomplete or misguided. This cognitive shortcut can be useful for quick decisions but dangerous in situations that demand careful consideration.

Another contributing factor is emotional attachment. When we become emotionally invested in a particular outcome or belief, we are less likely to entertain alternatives. This attachment creates a mental rigidity that resists change, even in the face of compelling evidence.

The philosopher Arthur Schopenhauer once observed, *"Every man takes the limits of his own field of vision for the limits of the world."* This observation highlights the insidious nature of tunnel vision: it convinces us that our narrow perspective is comprehensive, blinding us to broader possibilities.

Techniques for Stepping Back

Overcoming tunnel vision begins with cultivating the habit of stepping back—a deliberate
pause to reassess, reflect, and widen the frame of
reference. This practice requires both humility
and discipline, as it often involves questioning
deeply held assumptions and acknowledging
the limitations of our perspective.

One powerful technique is to adopt the mindset
of an outsider. By imagining how someone from
a different background, culture, or discipline
might approach the same situation, we gain a
fresh perspective. This approach aligns with the
concept of "beginner's mind" in Zen Buddhism,
which encourages approaching each moment
with openness and curiosity, free from preconceived notions.

Consider the example of Steve Jobs, who revolutionized technology and design by drawing
inspiration from seemingly unrelated fields,
such as calligraphy and music. Jobs's ability to
step outside the conventional boundaries of his
industry allowed him to create products that

were not only functional but also beautiful and intuitive. His success illustrates how stepping back and considering diverse perspectives can lead to innovative solutions.

Another technique is to actively seek opposing viewpoints. Engaging with those who challenge your ideas—not to argue, but to understand— broadens your perspective and sharpens your critical thinking. This practice is particularly valuable in polarized environments, where tunnel vision often reinforces division.

The Role of Reflection and Reassessment

Reflection is another key tool for avoiding tunnel vision. By regularly revisiting decisions and thought processes, we create opportunities to identify blind spots and adjust our approach. Reflection allows us to step back from the immediacy of the moment, gaining clarity and perspective.

One practical way to incorporate reflection is through journaling. Writing about challenges, decisions, and thought patterns can reveal recurring themes and biases, providing insights that might otherwise go unnoticed. For example, a leader struggling with a contentious decision might journal about the factors influencing their choice, uncovering hidden assumptions or over-looked alternatives.

Reassessment is equally important, particularly in fast-changing environments. The willingness to revise strategies, adapt to new information, and abandon outdated ideas is a hallmark of ef-fective decision-making. As the economist John Maynard Keynes famously quipped, *"When the facts change, I change my mind. What do you do?"* This mindset of adaptability is the antidote to the rigidity that tunnel vision creates.

The Balance Between Focus and Flexibility

Avoiding tunnel vision does not mean abandon-ing focus altogether. In fact, focus is often neces-sary for achieving clarity and purpose. The key is to balance focus with flexibility—maintaining a clear direction while remaining open to alter-native paths.

This balance is evident in the practice of mind-fulness, which teaches individuals to anchor their attention in the present moment while remaining aware of the broader context. By cultivating this dual awareness, mindfulness helps prevent the narrow fixation that leads to tunnel vision.

In professional settings, this balance can be achieved through collaborative decision-making. Encouraging input from diverse team members ensures that multiple perspectives are considered, reducing the risk of groupthink. Similarly, periodic reviews of goals and strategies can help organizations stay aligned with their objectives while remaining responsive to change.

Breaking Free from the Tunnel

The process of avoiding tunnel vision is not a one-time effort but an ongoing practice. It requires vigilance, curiosity, and a commitment to continuous growth. By cultivating the habit of stepping back, seeking diverse perspectives, and reflecting on decisions, we develop the mental agility to navigate life's complexities with greater clarity and purpose.

Ultimately, breaking free from tunnel vision allows us to see the bigger picture—to appreciate the interconnectedness of our choices, the richness of alternative perspectives, and the boundless potential of the human mind. As the poet William Blake wrote, *"If the doors of perception were cleansed, everything would appear to man as it is, infinite."* By widening our perspective, we move closer to this infinite vision, embracing life with openness, understanding, and wisdom.

Applying Contextual Awareness

Awareness of context is like adjusting the focus on a camera lens: it transforms a blurred and incomplete picture into a sharp, comprehensive view. In every decision we make, every relationship we build, and every challenge we face, context shapes the meaning and potential outcomes. By actively cultivating contextual awareness, we not only improve our understanding of the world but also enhance our ability to respond with clarity, empathy, and purpose.

Context in Professional Decisions

In the world of business and leadership, contextual awareness is often the difference between success and failure. Decisions made in isolation—without regard for market trends, cultural nuances, or organizational dynamics—frequently backfire. Conversely, decisions grounded in a deep understanding of context are more likely to resonate and endure.

Consider the case of Howard Schultz, the former CEO of Starbucks, who transformed the company from a modest coffee retailer into a global phenomenon. Schultz's success was not merely a result of offering high-quality coffee; it stemmed from his ability to understand and respond to the context of consumer behavior. Observing the café culture in Italy, where coffeehouses were social hubs, Schultz envisioned Starbucks as more than a coffee shop—it would become a "third place" between home and work.

This context-driven approach informed everything from store design to customer service, creating an experience that resonated deeply with modern lifestyles. Schultz's ability to see beyond the product itself and consider the broader context of consumer needs highlights the transformative power of contextual awareness in decision-making.

Context in Relationships

In personal and professional relationships, contextual awareness fosters empathy and understanding. By considering the circumstances that shape another person's actions or attitudes, we move beyond surface-level judgments and connect on a deeper level.

Imagine a situation where a colleague misses a deadline. Without context, the immediate reaction might be frustration or blame. However, taking the time to understand the circumstances—whether they're dealing with a personal crisis, navigating conflicting priorities, or lacking necessary resources—reveals a more nuanced picture. This contextual awareness not only diffuses tension but also opens the door to collaboration and support.

The same principle applies to broader social issues. During the civil rights movement, Martin Luther King Jr. emphasized the importance of understanding the historical and systemic context of racial inequality. In his famous "Letter from Birmingham Jail," King addressed criticisms of his methods by highlighting the context of centuries of oppression and systemic injustice. This perspective not only strengthened his argument but also invited others to view the issue through a broader lens, fostering empathy and solidarity.

Context in Societal Challenges

Contextual awareness is particularly critical in addressing complex societal challenges, where solutions require a comprehensive understanding of interconnected systems. Climate change, for example, cannot be tackled solely as an environmental issue; it is also a social, economic, and political challenge.

One striking example is the Paris Agreement, an international treaty aimed at combatting climate change. The success of this agreement depended on recognizing the diverse contexts of participating nations. Developed countries, with their historical responsibility for emissions, committed to providing financial and technological support to developing nations, which faced unique vulnerabilities to climate change. By accounting for these contextual differences, the agreement created a framework that acknowledged shared responsibility while addressing disparities in resources and capacity.

This same principle applies to local initiatives. A community working to reduce carbon emissions might focus on public transportation in urban areas while prioritizing sustainable agriculture in rural regions. Understanding the unique context of each setting ensures that solutions are both relevant and effective.

Practical Applications of Contextual Awareness

Developing contextual awareness begins with cultivating curiosity and asking the right questions. When faced with a decision or challenge, pause to consider:

- *What are the broader forces shaping this situation?*

- *How might historical or cultural factors influence outcomes?*

- *What perspectives or voices might I be missing?*

One practical strategy is to engage in systems thinking—a method of analyzing how different components of a system interact and influence one another. For example, a nonprofit organization addressing homelessness might consider not only immediate needs like shelter and food but also systemic factors such as affordable housing policies, mental health resources, and employment opportunities. By viewing the issue holistically, the organization can design interventions that address root causes rather than symptoms.

Another approach is to embrace interdisciplinary learning. By exploring fields outside your expertise, you gain insights that enrich your understanding of context. For instance, a healthcare professional studying sociology might develop a deeper appreciation for how social determinants like education and income shape health outcomes.

The Interplay of Context and Clarity

Contextual awareness and clarity are deeply intertwined. Understanding the broader picture sharpens our focus, enabling us to act with greater precision and purpose. This interplay is evident in the practice of mindfulness, which encourages individuals to anchor themselves in the present moment while remaining attuned to the broader environment.

In leadership, this dual focus is essential. A leader must balance immediate priorities with long-term vision, considering not only the needs of their team but also the larger organizational and societal context. For example, a CEO implementing diversity initiatives might address immediate representation goals while also examining systemic barriers to inclusion within the company's culture and policies.

Reflection as a Tool for Contextual Awareness

Reflection is a powerful practice for deepening contextual awareness. By regularly revisiting decisions and experiences, you gain insights into the factors that shaped them and identify opportunities for growth.

Consider a project that did not go as planned. Instead of focusing solely on the outcome, reflect on the context: *What external factors influenced the result? Were there underlying assumptions or biases at play? How might the approach be adjusted in the future?* This reflective process not only enhances self-awareness but also builds the habit of thinking contextually.

The Transformative Power of Contextual Awareness

When we embrace contextual awareness, we unlock the ability to navigate complexity with grace and wisdom. We move beyond reactive thinking, seeing each decision, interaction, and challenge as part of a larger tapestry. This broader perspective not only improves outcomes but also fosters connection, empathy, and purpose.

As the philosopher John Dewey observed, *"Knowledge of the past and its traditions can be emancipatory, opening the way to knowledge of the present and insight into what is to be done."* By understanding context, we gain the clarity to act not only in the moment but also in ways that resonate far into the future.

CHAPTER 4: SHIFTING PERSPECTIVES – WALKING IN OTHERS' SHOES

The Value of Empathy in Perspective

Empathy is the bridge between perception and understanding. It allows us to step beyond our personal experiences and view the world through the eyes of another. In doing so, empathy enriches our understanding of people, situations, and challenges, transforming not only how we see others but also how we relate to them. It is the cornerstone of meaningful relationships, effective leadership, and enduring conflict resolution.

Empathy as a Lens for Understanding

At its core, empathy is the ability to sense and share the emotions and experiences of others. It requires more than intellectual comprehension; it demands an emotional resonance that connects us to the struggles, joys, and complexities of another's life. Philosopher Martin Buber distinguished between two kinds of relationships: *I-It* and *I-Thou*. The former treats others as objects to be categorized and utilized, while the latter views them as unique individuals worthy of connection and respect. Empathy transforms relationships from *I-It* to *I-Thou*, creating bonds that transcend transactional interactions.

In practice, empathy shifts perspective in profound ways. Imagine a tense disagreement with a colleague. Without empathy, the conflict remains a battle of competing viewpoints, with neither party truly hearing the other. With empathy, however, the dynamic changes. By seeking to understand the colleague's concerns and motivations, you gain insight into their perspective, uncovering common ground and potential solutions. Empathy does not guarantee agreement, but it fosters a shared understanding that softens defenses and opens the door to collaboration.

The Role of Empathy in Leadership

Empathy has long been recognized as a hallmark of effective leadership. Leaders who cultivate empathy inspire trust, loyalty, and motivation, creating environments where individuals feel valued and understood. Empathy enables leaders to address challenges with sensitivity, balance competing priorities, and navigate crises with grace.

One striking historical example is Abraham Lincoln, whose presidency during the American Civil War required exceptional emotional intelligence. Lincoln's ability to empathize with opposing viewpoints, even those of his adversaries, allowed him to lead with both strength and compassion. His second inaugural address, delivered as the war drew to a close, exemplifies this empathy. Rather than vilifying the Confederacy, Lincoln urged the nation to heal "with malice toward none, with charity for all." This perspective not only reflected his understanding of the broader context but also inspired a vision of reconciliation that resonated deeply with his contemporaries.

In modern contexts, empathy continues to shape exemplary leadership. Satya Nadella, CEO of Microsoft, transformed the company's culture by emphasizing empathy as a core value. Nadella's leadership style focuses on understanding the needs of employees, customers, and stakeholders, fostering a culture of collaboration and innovation. Under his guidance, Microsoft has not only achieved remarkable financial success but also earned a reputation for inclusivity and social responsibility.

Empathy in Conflict Resolution

Empathy is particularly powerful in resolving conflicts, where opposing viewpoints often lead to entrenched positions and escalating tensions. By enabling individuals to see beyond their own perspective, empathy paves the way for dialogue, compromise, and mutual understanding.

The story of Nelson Mandela offers a profound illustration. After 27 years of imprisonment under South Africa's apartheid regime, Mandela emerged not with vengeance but with a vision of unity. His empathy for both Black South Africans, who suffered under apartheid, and white South Africans, who feared retribution, allowed him to lead the nation toward reconciliation. Mandela's ability to understand and address the fears and aspirations of both groups was instrumental in preventing a descent into civil war.

Empathy also plays a crucial role in everyday conflicts. In personal relationships, misunderstandings often stem from assumptions and misinterpretations. For instance, a disagreement

between friends might arise when one feels neglected while the other is preoccupied with personal challenges. Without empathy, the conflict
may escalate into resentment. With empathy,
both parties can recognize each other's emotions and needs, paving the way for resolution
and deeper connection.

Practical Benefits of Empathy

Beyond its moral and relational significance,
empathy offers practical advantages that enhance decision-making and problem-solving.
By understanding the perspectives of others, we
gain access to diverse insights and ideas, broadening our approach to challenges.

In business, this principle is evident in custom-
er-centric strategies. Companies that prioritize
understanding their customers' needs and desires often outperform competitors. For example,
design firm IDEO is renowned for its empathic
approach to innovation. By immersing themselves in the lives of users, IDEO's designers
uncover unmet needs and create products that
resonate deeply with consumers. This empathy-driven process has led to groundbreaking

innovations in healthcare, education, and technology.

On a societal level, empathy fosters cooperation and cohesion. In diverse communities, empathy helps bridge cultural divides, creating a shared sense of purpose and belonging. It also drives social progress by highlighting injustices and inspiring collective action. The abolition of slavery, the civil rights movement, and the fight for gender equality all emerged from the ability to empathize with the suffering of others and envision a more just world.

Cultivating Empathy

While empathy is often seen as an innate quality, it can be cultivated through deliberate practice. One of the simplest yet most profound ways to develop empathy is through active listening. By giving others our full attention, suspending judgment, and seeking to understand their experiences, we create space for authentic connection.

Another powerful practice is perspective-taking—the intentional effort to imagine how another person might feel in a given situation. This can be as simple as reflecting on a friend's challenges or as complex as exploring the lived experiences of individuals from different cultures or backgrounds.

Stories also play a vital role in fostering empathy. Literature, film, and art invite us into the lives of others, allowing us to experience their joys and struggles vicariously. As we immerse ourselves in these narratives, we expand our capacity to understand and connect with diverse perspectives.

The Transformative Power of Empathy

Empathy is more than a tool for understanding others; it is a transformative force that reshapes how we engage with the world. By walking in others' shoes, we not only deepen our connections but also unlock new perspectives that enrich our own lives. Empathy challenges us to see beyond our individual concerns, embracing the complexity and richness of the human experience.

As the philosopher and writer Maya Angelou

observed, *"I think we all have empathy. We may not have enough courage to display it."* Cultivating empathy requires that courage—the courage to listen, to understand, and to care. Yet, in doing so, we discover a profound truth: empathy is not only a gift we give to others but also a source of clarity and purpose in our own lives.

Overcoming Barriers to Empathy

While empathy has the power to transform relationships and deepen understanding, it is not always easy to access. Various barriers—both internal and external—can hinder our ability to connect with others on a meaningful level. These obstacles, rooted in egocentrism, cultural differences, and emotional defensiveness, often act as blinders, narrowing our perspective and reinforcing divisions. However, by identifying and addressing these barriers, we can cultivate the open-mindedness necessary to bridge gaps and build authentic connections.

The Weight of Egocentrism

Egocentrism, or the tendency to view the world primarily through one's own perspective, is perhaps the most pervasive barrier to empathy. This self-centered lens often leads us to prioritize our own needs, experiences, and emotions, leaving little room to consider those of others. While egocentrism is a natural aspect of human cognition—particularly in childhood—it becomes problematic when left unchecked in adulthood.

Imagine a workplace scenario where a manager assumes their team members should approach challenges in the same way they do. Without considering the diverse experiences and working styles of their team, the manager's decisions may inadvertently alienate others or stifle creativity. This lack of perspective not only undermines morale but also limits the potential for innovation and collaboration.

Overcoming egocentrism requires intentional effort to step outside oneself. The philosopher Immanuel Kant offered a guiding principle: *"Act only according to that maxim whereby you can, at the same time, will that it should become a universal law."* This moral framework challenges us to consider how our actions and beliefs might impact others, encouraging a shift from self-interest to collective well-being.

Practical strategies for addressing egocentrism include mindfulness practices that foster self-awareness and active listening techniques that prioritize the voices of others. By creating space to truly hear and understand those around us, we begin to dismantle the barriers of self-centered thinking.

Navigating Cultural Differences

Cultural differences can also present significant challenges to empathy. These differences shape values, communication styles, and worldviews, often leading to misunderstandings or misinterpretations. While diversity enriches our interactions, it can also create friction when assumptions and biases go unexamined.

Consider the story of the first encounter between Japanese and American negotiators during trade talks in the mid-20th century. The American delegation, accustomed to direct and assertive communication, misinterpreted the Japanese team's indirect responses as evasive or uncommitted. Meanwhile, the Japanese delegation viewed the Americans' assertiveness as overly aggressive. These cultural differences, left unaddressed, initially hindered progress and mutual understanding.

To overcome such barriers, it is essential to approach cultural differences with curiosity and humility. Anthropologist Edward T. Hall emphasized the importance of understanding cultural contexts, noting that "communication is culture and culture is communication." By learning about the values, norms, and traditions of others, we gain insight into the frameworks that shape their behavior.

Additionally, practicing cultural relativism — the ability to view another culture's practices within its own context rather than through the lens of one's own — can help foster empathy. For example, rather than judging a collectivist culture's emphasis on group harmony as suppressive, one might appreciate it as a value that prioritizes interconnectedness and mutual support.

The Wall of Emotional Defensiveness

Emotional defensiveness often arises when we feel threatened, judged, or vulnerable. In such moments, our instinct is to protect ourselves, which can make it difficult to empathize with others. Defensiveness manifests as dismissiveness, blame-shifting, or an unwillingness to engage with perspectives that challenge our own.

One striking example of emotional defensiveness can be seen in the history of the civil rights movement in the United States. As activists fought for racial equality, many white Americans reacted defensively, interpreting calls for change as personal attacks on their character or way of life. This defensiveness often obscured the real issues of systemic injustice, delaying progress and deepening divides.

To overcome emotional defensiveness, it is crucial to develop emotional resilience—the ability to sit with discomfort and remain open to dialogue. Psychologist Carl Rogers advocated for "unconditional positive regard," a practice that involves accepting others without judgment while maintaining a sense of self-worth. This approach creates a safe space for empathy to flourish, even in the face of challenging conversations.

Practically, this might involve pausing before
responding to perceived criticism, reflecting
on the emotions driving the defensiveness, and
reframing the situation as an opportunity for
growth. For instance, if a friend expresses dissatisfaction with a behavior, rather than reacting
with denial or justification, one might respond
with curiosity: *"Can you help me understand how
you felt in that moment?"* This openness transforms conflict into connection.

Cultivating Open-Mindedness

At the heart of overcoming barriers to empathy
is the cultivation of open-mindedness—a willingness to explore unfamiliar perspectives and
entertain ideas that challenge our assumptions.
Open-mindedness requires humility, recognizing that our understanding is always partial and
subject to refinement.

One practice that fosters open-mindedness is
engaging with stories. Literature, film, and art
offer windows into the experiences of others,
allowing us to inhabit perspectives we might

never encounter in daily life. For example, reading Chimamanda Ngozi Adichie's *Half of a Yellow Sun* provides insight into the Nigerian Civil War, while watching a documentary on climate refugees reveals the human impact of environmental change. These narratives expand our empathetic imagination, preparing us to approach real-world interactions with greater sensitivity.

Another powerful tool is dialogue. Seeking out conversations with individuals who hold different views—whether on politics, religion, or personal values—broadens our understanding and challenges biases. However, such dialogues must be approached with genuine curiosity and respect, prioritizing listening over debating.

The Rewards of Breaking Barriers

When we overcome the barriers to empathy, the rewards are profound. Relationships become richer, conflicts are resolved more effectively, and decision-making becomes more inclusive and thoughtful. Empathy not only enhances individual connections but also fosters societal cohesion, creating communities that are resilient, compassionate, and united.

As the Dalai Lama observed, *"Empathy is the most precious human quality."* It is a quality that transcends differences, bridging divides and illuminating the shared humanity that binds us all. By addressing the barriers that hinder empathy, we unlock its transformative power, enabling us to walk in others' shoes and see the world through their eyes.

Techniques for Perspective-Taking

Perspective-taking is the deliberate act of stepping into another's shoes, seeing the world through their eyes, and understanding their thoughts, emotions, and motivations. It is a skill that bridges the gap between self and other, deepening connections and fostering mutual understanding. Yet, like any skill, it requires practice and intention to master. By employing techniques such as reflective listening, role-playing, and embracing opposing viewpoints, we can cultivate the ability to engage with diverse perspectives effectively and compassionately.

Reflective Listening: Hearing Beyond Words

Reflective listening is more than hearing; it is a way of truly understanding another person's experience. At its core, reflective listening involves attentively listening to someone, then summarizing or paraphrasing their message to confirm understanding. This technique not only clarifies communication but also demonstrates empathy, signaling that the speaker's perspective is valued and respected.

Consider a conversation between two colleagues with differing opinions on a project. Without reflective listening, the dialogue may quickly devolve into arguments, with each party focusing solely on defending their position. With reflective listening, however, the dynamic shifts. One colleague might say, *"If I understand you correctly, you're concerned that my approach might overlook potential risks. Is that right?"* This reflection acknowledges the concern, fostering trust and opening the door to collaborative problem-solving.

The value of reflective listening extends beyond individual interactions. It has been a cornerstone of effective mediation and conflict resolution for centuries. In ancient Greece, Socrates employed a similar method in his dialogues, asking questions and paraphrasing responses to deepen understanding and uncover truth. Today, reflective listening remains a vital tool for bridging divides, from personal relationships to international diplomacy.

Role-Playing: Walking in Their Shoes

Role-playing is a powerful technique for perspective-taking, enabling individuals to experience a situation from another person's viewpoint. By temporarily adopting someone else's role, we gain insights into their challenges, emotions, and motivations that might otherwise remain inaccessible.

One notable example comes from the education sector, where role-playing exercises are often used to address issues like bullying and cultural sensitivity. Students might be asked to assume the roles of individuals from different backgrounds, exploring how prejudice, privilege, or marginalization shapes their experiences. These exercises not only build empathy but also equip participants with the tools to navigate real-world interactions with greater awareness and compassion.

In professional settings, role-playing can be equally transformative. A manager preparing for a difficult conversation with an employee might practice the exchange with a colleague, playing the role of the employee to anticipate their concerns and emotions. This preparation allows the manager to approach the conversation with greater sensitivity, fostering a more constructive outcome.

Philosophically, role-playing aligns with the teachings of Jean-Paul Sartre, who emphasized the importance of recognizing others as conscious beings with their own realities. By engaging in role-playing, we momentarily set aside our own perspective, stepping into the relational dynamic that Sartre described as *being-for-others*.

Adopting Opposing Viewpoints: Expanding the Horizon

One of the most challenging yet rewarding techniques for perspective-taking is adopting opposing viewpoints. This practice involves setting aside personal beliefs to explore and articulate an alternative perspective, not to agree with it but to understand its logic and emotional underpinnings.

In the realm of law, this technique is fundamental. Lawyers are trained to anticipate and counter opposing arguments, requiring them to think critically from multiple angles. This skill is not limited to the courtroom; it is equally valuable in everyday life. For instance, a parent debating bedtime rules with their teenager might pause to consider the teenager's perspective: *Why do they value staying up later? What unmet needs might this preference reflect?* By understanding the opposing viewpoint, the parent can craft a solution that balances both priorities.

The practice of adopting opposing viewpoints has been championed by figures like John Stuart Mill, who argued that engaging with dissenting opinions strengthens our own understanding. In his seminal work, *On Liberty*, Mill asserted that encountering opposing perspectives prevents dogmatism and encourages intellectual growth.

Practically, this technique can be cultivated through dialogue or even self-reflection. When encountering a differing opinion, instead of reacting defensively, pause to explore its merits: *What might this person see that I do not? How does their experience shape this belief?* This shift in mindset transforms disagreement into an opportunity for learning.

The Role of Imagination in Perspective-Taking

Imagination is a subtle yet powerful tool for perspective-taking. It allows us to transcend the boundaries of our direct experience, envisioning scenarios, emotions, and realities that differ from our own. The novelist George Eliot captured this sentiment beautifully when she wrote, *"The greatest benefit we owe to the artist, whether painter, poet, or novelist, is the extension of our sympathies."*

Literature, art, and film serve as conduits for this imaginative process. A reader immersing themselves in a novel like *To Kill a Mockingbird* experiences life through the eyes of Scout, a child witnessing racial injustice in the American

South. This vicarious perspective fosters empathy, revealing truths about society and human nature that resonate beyond the page.

Incorporating imaginative exercises into daily life can also enhance perspective-taking. For example, when faced with a conflict, take a moment to visualize the other person's experience in vivid detail. Imagine their day, their stressors, and their motivations. This imaginative leap, though simple, often illuminates nuances that might otherwise remain hidden.

Balancing Perspective with Authenticity

While perspective-taking expands understanding, it is important to balance this openness with authenticity. The goal is not to lose oneself in another's perspective but to integrate it into a more comprehensive view of the situation. This balance requires self-awareness—recognizing where your perspective ends and another's begins, and finding harmony between the two.

Consider the role of a mediator facilitating a negotiation. The mediator must empathize with both parties, understanding their needs and grievances, without becoming biased or losing sight of the broader goal. This balance of perspective and authenticity is the essence of effective perspective-taking: it honors the complexity of human experience while maintaining clarity of purpose.

The Transformative Impact of Perspective-Taking

When practiced consistently, perspective-taking transforms how we engage with the world. It enriches relationships by fostering trust and understanding, enhances problem-solving by revealing diverse solutions, and deepens self-awareness by challenging assumptions. In a world often divided by misunderstanding, perspective-taking serves as a unifying force, bridging gaps and celebrating diversity.

Ultimately, perspective-taking is not just a skill but a way of being—a commitment to seeing others not as obstacles or opponents but as fellow travelers on the journey of life. As the philosopher Martha Nussbaum observed, *"Compassion requires the ability to see the world from another's perspective."* By cultivating this ability, we unlock the potential for compassion, connection, and shared purpose.

Empathy in Action

Empathy, when translated into action, becomes a powerful force for resolving conflicts, strengthening relationships, and fostering collaboration. By stepping into another's shoes and viewing the world through their eyes, we unlock new possibilities for understanding and connection. The true measure of empathy lies not in intention but in its application—in how it transforms interactions, decisions, and outcomes.

Throughout history, empathy has driven some of the most profound resolutions to seemingly insurmountable conflicts. In modern contexts, it continues to serve as a bridge between opposing viewpoints, enabling individuals and groups to navigate complexity with grace and humanity.

Empathy in Leadership: Nelson Mandela's Vision

One of the most striking examples of empathy in action is Nelson Mandela's leadership during South Africa's transition from apartheid to democracy. After spending 27 years in prison, Mandela emerged not with bitterness but with a commitment to reconciliation. He understood that building a unified nation required address-ing the fears and grievances of both Black and white South Africans.

Mandela's empathetic approach was evident in his decision to establish the Truth and Recon-ciliation Commission (TRC), which invited vic-tims and perpetrators of apartheid-era crimes to share their stories. This process was not about retribution but about acknowledgment, healing, and understanding. By creating a space where both sides could express their pain and seek forgiveness, Mandela fostered a sense of shared humanity that was essential for rebuilding the nation.

Mandela's empathy extended beyond grand gestures. In a symbolic act, he invited Percy Yutar, the prosecutor who had argued for his imprisonment, to lunch. This willingness to engage with adversaries on a personal level reflected Mandela's belief in the transformative power of understanding. His empathy was not

passive; it was active, deliberate, and transformative, guiding South Africa toward peace and
unity.

Resolving Everyday Conflicts Through Empathy

While Mandela's story illustrates empathy on
a national scale, its principles apply equally to
everyday conflicts. Whether in personal relationships, workplaces, or communities, empathy-driven perspective-taking can de-escalate
tensions and foster solutions.

Consider a disagreement between two friends—
one feels neglected because the other has been
unresponsive. Without empathy, the situation
might escalate into blame or defensiveness, further straining the relationship. With empathy,
however, the dynamic changes. By seeking to
understand the other's perspective, the friends
might uncover underlying factors: one is struggling with a demanding workload, while the
other feels vulnerable and in need of support.
This mutual understanding allows them to address the root of the issue and find ways to
reconnect.

In workplaces, empathy is equally transformative. Imagine a manager addressing an underperforming employee. Instead of issuing reprimands, the manager takes the time to understand the employee's challenges—perhaps they are dealing with personal stress or unclear expectations. This empathetic approach not only resolves the immediate issue but also strengthens trust and morale, fostering a more positive and productive environment.

Empathy in Negotiation and Diplomacy

Empathy is a cornerstone of successful negotiation and diplomacy, where understanding the other party's interests and motivations is essential for finding common ground.

The 1978 Camp David Accords, brokered by U.S. President Jimmy Carter, offer a compelling example. This historic agreement between Egypt and Israel marked a major step toward peace in the Middle East. Carter's approach was rooted in empathy—he sought to understand the fears, desires, and cultural contexts of both leaders, Egyptian President Anwar Sadat and Israeli

Prime Minister Menachem Begin.

By addressing these underlying concerns, Carter facilitated a dialogue that transcended surface-level disputes. He personally connected with both leaders, even going so far as to appeal to their shared humanity through stories of his own life and family. This empathy-driven approach created the trust necessary for compromise, resulting in a peace treaty that endures to this day.

Building Stronger Relationships Through Empathy

Empathy strengthens relationships by fostering trust, communication, and mutual respect. When individuals feel understood and valued, they are more likely to open up, collaborate, and invest in the relationship.

In family dynamics, for instance, empathy helps bridge generational divides. A parent struggling to connect with a teenager might initially view their behavior as rebellious or dismissive. By approaching the situation with empathy—seeking to understand the pressures, insecurities, and aspirations driving the teenager's actions—the parent gains insight that transforms the relationship. Instead of enforcing authority, the parent becomes a trusted ally, fostering open communication and mutual respect.

Romantic relationships also thrive on empathy. Research in psychology highlights the importance of empathic attunement—the ability to sense and respond to a partner's emotional needs. Couples who practice empathy are better equipped to navigate conflicts, as they prioritize understanding over winning. This shift from adversarial to collaborative problem-solving strengthens the bond and creates a foundation for long-term connection.

The Ripple Effect of Empathy

The impact of empathy extends beyond individual interactions, creating ripple effects that transform communities and societies. When empathy becomes a cultural value, it fosters inclusion, reduces prejudice, and inspires collective action.

One modern example is the global response to

the Syrian refugee crisis. While political debates often focused on logistics and security, many grassroots organizations and individuals approached the issue with empathy. They sought to understand the refugees' experiences—families displaced by war, children deprived of education, individuals risking everything for safety. This empathetic perspective drove initiatives that provided shelter, education, and advocacy, demonstrating the power of compassion to effect meaningful change.

Empathy also drives social justice movements. From the fight for civil rights in the United States to the global movement for LGBTQ+ equality, empathy has been the foundation of progress. By amplifying the voices of marginalized communities and inviting others to see the world through their eyes, these movements challenge indifference and inspire action.

Empathy as a Practice

While empathy is a natural human capacity, it requires conscious cultivation to reach its full potential. This involves not only developing skills like active listening and perspective-taking but also creating environments that nurture empathy.

Schools, workplaces, and communities can promote empathy by fostering dialogue, celebrating diversity, and encouraging acts of kindness. Storytelling is a particularly powerful tool in this regard. By sharing narratives that illuminate different experiences, we build bridges of understanding that connect even the most disparate perspectives.

As individuals, we can practice empathy by approaching interactions with curiosity and humility. Instead of rushing to judgment or assumptions, we can ask questions like, *What might this person be experiencing? What fears or hopes are shaping their behavior?* This simple shift transforms everyday interactions into opportunities for connection and growth.

The Transformative Power of Empathy in Action

Empathy in action is a force that transcends boundaries, resolves conflicts, and builds stronger relationships. It is not merely an abstract ideal but a practical tool for navigating the complexities of human interaction. As we integrate empathy into our daily lives, we unlock its transformative power, creating a world that is not only more understanding but also more compassionate.

The Dalai Lama reminds us, *"Only the development of compassion and understanding for others can bring us the tranquility and happiness we all seek."* By putting empathy into action, we contribute to this vision—one relationship, one interaction, and one act of understanding at a time.

CHAPTER 5: THE CLARITY-ACTION LINK – TRANSFORMING VISION INTO RESULTS

Clarity as a Catalyst for Action

Clarity is the spark that ignites purposeful action. When our thoughts are muddled, and our priorities obscured, progress falters. But with clarity, the path forward becomes unmistakable, and the energy required to act flows naturally. In both personal and professional realms, the connection between clear thinking and effective action is profound. Clarity dissolves the barriers of indecision and distraction, replacing them with focus, confidence, and momentum.

The Power of Focused Thinking

Clarity sharpens focus by distilling complexity into manageable parts. It provides a sense of direction, allowing us to navigate challenges without succumbing to overwhelm. Imagine a traveler standing at the edge of a dense forest, unsure which path to take. Without a clear sense of direction, each step becomes fraught with uncertainty, and progress slows. Now imagine that same traveler equipped with a map and a compass. Suddenly, the journey becomes purposeful, each step taken with intention and confidence.

This metaphor illustrates the role of clarity in action. It transforms uncertainty into decisiveness, enabling us to allocate our time and energy toward meaningful goals. The psychologist Mihaly Csikszentmihalyi, known for his work on the concept of "flow," observed that focused attention is key to achieving a state of deep engagement. When our goals are clear, we enter a flow state where action feels effortless and outcomes are optimized.

Historical Lessons: Clarity in Leadership

History offers countless examples of how clarity has empowered individuals to achieve extraordinary results. One such figure is Mahatma Gandhi, whose clear vision of nonviolent resistance galvanized an entire nation. Gandhi's approach to India's independence movement was rooted in simplicity and focus. He distilled his message into principles that resonated universally — truth, nonviolence, and self-reliance.

This clarity of purpose not only inspired millions but also provided a framework for sustained action. Gandhi's ability to articulate his vision with unwavering conviction eliminated ambiguity and rallied diverse groups toward a common goal. His leadership exemplifies how clarity serves as both a personal and collective catalyst for transformation.

Eliminating Indecision

Indecision is often the result of competing priorities, unresolved doubts, or fear of making the wrong choice. Clarity neutralizes these obstacles by illuminating what truly matters. When we take the time to reflect on our values and goals, the noise of distraction fades, and the essential becomes apparent.

Consider the example of Marie Curie, the pioneering scientist who became the first woman to win a Nobel Prize. Curie's groundbreaking work on radioactivity required immense focus and dedication. Faced with limited resources, societal skepticism, and personal challenges, she maintained her commitment to scientific discovery. Curie's clarity of purpose—her unwavering belief in the potential of her research—enabled her to persevere despite overwhelming odds.

On a smaller scale, the same principle applies to daily decision-making. Imagine a student struggling to balance academic responsibilities with social commitments. Without clarity, they might oscillate between choices, accomplishing little in either area. By identifying their priorities—whether achieving academic success or cultivating meaningful relationships—they can make deliberate decisions that align with their goals, eliminating the paralysis of indecision.

Practical Steps to Cultivate Clarity for Action

Clarity is not an inherent trait but a skill that can be cultivated through deliberate practice. One powerful method is the practice of reflection. Taking time to journal, meditate, or simply pause to assess your thoughts and goals can provide invaluable insights. Ask yourself:

- *What am I trying to achieve?*

- *What obstacles are standing in my way?*

- *What steps can I take today to move closer to my goal?*

Another effective approach is to simplify complexity. In today's fast-paced world, it is easy to become overwhelmed by the sheer volume of information and options. By breaking tasks into smaller, actionable steps, you reduce the cognitive load and create a clear roadmap for progress. For example, rather than setting an abstract goal like "get healthy," focus on specific actions such as walking 10,000 steps daily or preparing nutritious meals.

Visualization is also a powerful tool for clarity. By imagining the desired outcome in vivid detail, you reinforce your commitment to achieving it. Athletes, entrepreneurs, and performers alike use visualization to prime their minds for success, translating abstract goals into concrete mental images that guide their actions.

The Interplay Between Clarity and Motivation

Clarity not only drives action but also sustains motivation. When we understand why we are pursuing a goal, the effort required becomes meaningful rather than burdensome. This connection between clarity and motivation is evident in the story of the Apollo 11 mission.

In 1961, President John F. Kennedy declared the ambitious goal of landing a man on the moon before the decade's end. This vision was both clear and inspiring, galvanizing NASA scientists, engineers, and astronauts to achieve what had previously seemed impossible. By breaking the mission into manageable phases and articulating a compelling purpose—advancing human exploration—Kennedy's clarity provided the foundation for one of history's greatest achievements.

Clarity in Personal Growth

Clarity is equally transformative in personal growth. When we align our actions with our core values and long-term aspirations, we create a sense of harmony and fulfillment. For example, an individual seeking to develop a new skill might begin by identifying their motivations— whether personal enrichment, career advancement, or creative expression. This clarity not only informs the choice of skill but also guides the learning process, ensuring that each step feels purposeful.

In relationships, clarity fosters authenticity and connection. By understanding your own needs and communicating them openly, you create space for meaningful dialogue and mutual understanding. For instance, a couple navigating a challenging period might use clarity to articulate their shared goals—whether rebuilding trust, improving communication, or supporting each other's growth. This shared vision becomes a guiding light, illuminating the path forward.

The Ripple Effect of Clear Thinking

The impact of clarity extends beyond individual actions, creating a ripple effect that influences those around us. When leaders, parents, or mentors act with clarity, they inspire others to do the same. This ripple effect fosters a culture of purpose and intentionality, where individuals and communities thrive.

As the Roman philosopher Seneca observed, *"If a man knows not to which port he sails, no wind is favorable."* Clarity provides the direction we need to harness life's opportunities, transforming potential into results. By cultivating clarity in thought and action, we unlock the power to navigate challenges, achieve goals, and live with purpose.

Goal Setting Through Clarity

Setting goals is a fundamental aspect of translating vision into action. Yet, goals that are vague, misaligned with values, or overly ambitious can lead to frustration and stagnation. Clarity transforms goal setting from an abstract exercise into a purposeful process, ensuring that each objective serves as a stepping stone toward a larger vision. By aligning goals with personal values and long-term aspirations, we create a roadmap that is not only achievable but also deeply meaningful.

The Power of Clear Goals

Clear goals provide direction and structure. Without them, our efforts risk being scattered, reactive, or unfocused. A clear goal acts as a guiding star, orienting our actions and decisions toward a defined outcome. This clarity reduces uncertainty, allowing us to channel our energy effectively.

One illustrative example comes from the field of aviation. In the 1950s, Dr. Edwin Locke, a pioneering psychologist, conducted research that highlighted the importance of clear, specific goals in improving performance. He found that individuals who set specific objectives—such as increasing speed or reducing errors—outperformed those with vague intentions like "doing their best." This principle, now known as goal-setting theory, underscores the transformative impact of clarity on achievement.

On a personal level, clear goals act as a source of motivation. Consider an aspiring writer who dreams of publishing a novel. Without clarity, this dream might remain a nebulous ambition. But by breaking it down into specific goals—such as writing 1,000 words daily or completing a chapter each month—the writer creates a framework for progress. Each milestone builds momentum, transforming the abstract goal into a tangible reality.

Aligning Goals with Personal Values

While clarity enhances focus, alignment with

personal values ensures that goals remain meaningful. Misaligned goals—those driven by external expectations or fleeting desires—often lead to dissatisfaction, even when achieved. In contrast, goals rooted in core values resonate deeply, fostering a sense of purpose and fulfillment.

The story of Viktor Frankl, a Holocaust survivor and renowned psychiatrist, illustrates this principle. In his seminal work, *Man's Search for Meaning*, Frankl observed that individuals who pursued goals aligned with their values were more resilient and fulfilled, even in the face of unimaginable adversity. For Frankl, the pursuit of meaning—whether through relationships, work, or self-transcendence—was the ultimate motivator.

To align goals with values, begin by reflecting on what matters most to you. Ask yourself:

- *What do I want my life to stand for?*

- *What activities or achievements bring me the deepest sense of satisfaction?*

- How do my goals contribute to the well-being of others?

This alignment transforms goal setting into an exercise in authenticity. For example, an entrepreneur whose core value is environmental sustainability might prioritize goals such as developing eco-friendly products or reducing their company's carbon footprint. This alignment ensures that their professional achievements resonate with their personal ethos.

The Importance of Long-Term Vision

While short-term goals provide immediate focus, they are most effective when anchored to a long-term vision. This vision serves as a compass, ensuring that each short-term objective contributes to a larger purpose. Without it, even clear goals can feel fragmented or aimless.

Consider the Apollo program, which culminated in the 1969 moon landing. The success of this ambitious endeavor was rooted in a long-term vision articulated by President John F. Kennedy: landing a man on the moon and returning him safely to Earth. This vision provided a unifying purpose, guiding the efforts of thousands of scientists, engineers, and astronauts. Each short-term goal—whether developing rocket technology or conducting spacewalks—was aligned with the ultimate objective, ensuring cohesive progress.

For individuals, cultivating a long-term vision involves envisioning the life you want to create. What legacy do you hope to leave? What contributions do you want to make? By answering these questions, you create a framework for setting short-term goals that are both meaningful and strategic.

Methods for Setting Achievable Goals

Once clarity and alignment are established, the next step is to translate vision into actionable goals. One effective method is the SMART framework, which emphasizes goals that are Specific, Measurable, Achievable, Relevant, and Time-bound. While this approach is widely used in professional settings, it is equally applicable to personal aspirations.

For example, instead of setting a vague goal like

"get in shape," a SMART goal might be: "Run three times per week and complete a 5K race within six months." This specificity not only enhances focus but also provides benchmarks for tracking progress.

Another method is reverse engineering—starting with your long-term vision and working backward to identify the steps required to achieve it. For instance, an artist aiming to hold a gallery exhibition might outline intermediate goals such as building a portfolio, networking with curators, and securing funding. This process ensures that each step is purposeful and aligned with the larger objective.

Overcoming Common Pitfalls

Despite its benefits, goal setting is not without challenges. One common pitfall is setting goals that are overly ambitious, leading to burnout or discouragement. To avoid this, it is essential to balance ambition with realism. Ask yourself: *Is this goal challenging enough to inspire growth while remaining attainable?*

Another challenge is losing sight of goals amidst

daily distractions or setbacks. Regular reflection—whether through journaling, meditation, or discussions with a mentor—can help you stay connected to your objectives. Revisiting your "why"—the deeper purpose behind your goals—reinforces commitment and resilience.

The Ripple Effect of Goal Setting

Clear, aligned goals not only transform individual lives but also inspire and influence those around us. Leaders, parents, and mentors who model intentional goal setting create environments where others are empowered to do the same.

One striking example comes from Malala Yousafzai, the Nobel Peace Prize laureate and advocate for girls' education. Despite facing life-threatening opposition, Malala's clear and unwavering goal of promoting education for all has inspired millions worldwide. Her journey illustrates how a single individual's clarity and commitment can ignite collective action, creating ripples that extend far beyond their immediate circle.

The Journey of Clarity and Goals

Goal setting is not a one-time event but an ongoing journey. As circumstances change and new opportunities arise, goals must be reassessed and refined. This adaptability ensures that your objectives remain relevant and aligned with your evolving values and vision.

By setting clear, achievable goals, you create a bridge between intention and action. These goals serve as markers of progress, guiding you toward a life of purpose and fulfillment. As the poet Rainer Maria Rilke wrote, *"The purpose of life is to be defeated by greater and greater things."* By pursuing meaningful goals with clarity, you embrace this purpose, transforming challenges into opportunities for growth and discovery.

Overcoming Analysis Paralysis

In an age of endless information and boundless choices, analysis paralysis has become a common affliction. The term refers to the state of overthinking decisions to the point of inaction—a phenomenon where the search for the "perfect" choice prevents any choice from being made at all. While careful deliberation is valuable, excessive rumination often leads to frustration, missed opportunities, and unnecessary stress. Overcoming analysis paralysis requires cultivating a balance between thoughtfulness and decisiveness, embracing imperfection, and developing confidence in the face of uncertainty.

The Roots of Analysis Paralysis

Analysis paralysis stems from several psychological tendencies. One is the fear of making the wrong decision, driven by the desire to maximize outcomes and avoid regret. This fear can become magnified when decisions carry significant consequences, such as choosing a career path, a life partner, or a financial investment.

Another contributing factor is the overwhelming abundance of options in modern life. Psychologist Barry Schwartz explores this phenomenon in his book, *The Paradox of Choice*. Schwartz argues that while choice can empower individuals, an excess of options often leads to indecision, anxiety, and dissatisfaction. Faced with too many variables, the brain struggles to weigh pros and cons, creating a mental logjam.

Perfectionism also plays a role. The belief that every decision must lead to the optimal outcome can create unrealistic expectations, paralyzing individuals who fear falling short. Philosopher Voltaire famously warned against this mindset, observing, *"Perfect is the enemy of good."*

Historical Lessons: Acting Amid Uncertainty

History is replete with examples of leaders and innovators who overcame analysis paralysis to make decisive choices under uncertain circumstances. One such figure is Winston Churchill during World War II. As Prime Minister of Britain, Churchill faced constant pressure to make swift and high-stakes decisions, often with incomplete or conflicting information.

In May 1940, as Nazi Germany advanced through Europe, Churchill made the pivotal decision to evacuate British troops from Dunkirk. Despite the immense logistical challenges and uncertainty surrounding the operation's success, he acted decisively, ordering the deployment of civilian vessels to aid in the rescue effort. This decision, though fraught with risk, ultimately saved over 330,000 soldiers, preserving the strength of Britain's armed forces. Churchill's ability to weigh options quickly and commit to action highlights the importance of decisiveness in overcoming paralysis.

The Cost of Inaction

While overanalyzing decisions may feel like a way to ensure success, it often leads to missed opportunities and unintended consequences. Inaction itself is a decision—one that can carry significant costs. For example, an entrepreneur who spends years perfecting their product without launching risks losing market relevance, while an investor paralyzed by market fluctuations may miss opportunities for growth.

Moreover, analysis paralysis can erode confidence. The longer one hesitates, the more daunting the decision becomes, creating a feedback loop of doubt and delay. Breaking this cycle requires embracing imperfection and recognizing that action, even if imperfect, is often more valuable than inaction.

Strategies for Breaking Free from Paralysis

Overcoming analysis paralysis involves adopting practical strategies that balance reflection with action. One such strategy is setting clear decision-making criteria. By defining what matters most—whether it's cost, efficiency, or alignment with values—you create a framework that simplifies the evaluation process. For instance, a job seeker deciding between offers might prioritize factors like growth potential, company culture, and commute time, reducing the complexity of the choice.

Another effective approach is to impose deadlines. Deadlines create a sense of urgency, forcing decisions to be made within a defined timeframe. This technique is particularly useful in professional settings, where prolonged deliberation can stall progress. By committing to a decision by a specific date, you shift the focus from perfection to practicality.

Experimentation also offers a way to overcome indecision. Instead of committing to a single path, consider testing multiple options on a smaller scale. For example, an individual exploring career changes might take on freelance projects or volunteer opportunities to gain insight into different fields. This hands-on approach reduces the stakes of the decision, providing clarity through experience.

The Role of Intuition

While analysis often relies on logic and data, intuition plays a crucial role in decision-making. Intuition, or the "gut feeling," is not irrational; it is the brain's ability to draw on past experiences and subconscious knowledge to guide choices. Neuroscientist Antonio Damasio's research highlights the importance of emotional signals in decision-making, showing that individuals who lack access to these signals due to brain injuries struggle to make even simple choices.

Tapping into intuition requires trusting your instincts, particularly in situations where information is incomplete or contradictory. For example, a leader deciding whether to launch a new initiative might rely on their experience and understanding of market trends to make a call, even if data is inconclusive. While intuition should not replace analysis, it can complement it, providing a valuable counterbalance to overthinking.

Reframing Uncertainty as Opportunity

A key aspect of overcoming analysis paralysis is shifting your mindset about uncertainty. Rather than viewing uncertainty as a barrier, consider it an opportunity for growth and discovery. Philosopher Søren Kierkegaard described this as the "leap of faith"—the willingness to act without complete certainty, trusting that the journey itself will yield insight and meaning.

For example, an artist facing creative block might fear committing to a particular medium or theme, worrying it won't resonate with their audience. By reframing the decision as an experiment rather than a final verdict, they can free themselves from the weight of perfectionism, allowing creativity to flow.

Building Confidence Through Small Wins

Another powerful tool for breaking analysis paralysis is the pursuit of small wins. By taking incremental actions and achieving manageable successes, you build confidence and momentum. These small victories reinforce the belief that progress is possible, even in the face of uncertainty.

Consider a student overwhelmed by the prospect of writing a thesis. Rather than focusing on the daunting task as a whole, they might start by outlining one section or writing a single paragraph. Each completed step reinforces their ability to move forward, gradually transforming the seemingly insurmountable task into a series of achievable milestones.

The Balance Between Thought and Action

Overcoming analysis paralysis is not about abandoning thoughtfulness but about finding balance. By combining clear criteria, intuitive judgment, and decisive action, you create a process that respects complexity without succumbing to it. This balance is the essence of effective decision-making—a dynamic interplay between reflection and execution.

As the ancient Chinese philosopher Laozi observed, *"A journey of a thousand miles begins with a single step."* By embracing imperfection, acting with intention, and trusting the process, you can overcome the paralysis of overanalysis, transforming potential into progress and vision into results.

Sustaining Momentum

Momentum is the force that transforms initial clarity and decisive action into sustained progress. While setting clear goals and taking the first steps are vital, maintaining clarity and purpose during setbacks and challenges is what ultimately determines success. Momentum acts as a buffer against stagnation, propelling us forward even when obstacles arise. Cultivating this resilience requires a combination of strategic practices, emotional fortitude, and a deep connection to one's vision.

The Nature of Momentum

Momentum is self-reinforcing. Small successes build confidence, which in turn fuels further action. However, it is not immune to disruption. Life's uncertainties—unexpected setbacks, shifting priorities, or external challenges—can derail even the most focused efforts. Sustaining momentum means not only recovering from these disruptions but also using them as opportunities to reaffirm purpose and recalibrate strategies.

A powerful example comes from the life of Thomas Edison. The inventor of the lightbulb faced countless failures before achieving success. Famously, Edison conducted over 1,000 experiments before finding the right filament for his invention. When asked about his repeated failures, Edison reportedly replied, *"I have not failed. I've just found 10,000 ways that won't work."* This perspective highlights the importance of persistence and a clear vision in sustaining momentum. Each setback was not a defeat but a step closer to his ultimate goal.

Clarity as a Guide Through Challenges

Clarity serves as an anchor during turbulent times. When setbacks threaten to derail progress, reconnecting with the "why" behind your efforts provides the motivation to persevere. This principle is evident in the story of Rosa Parks, whose courageous act of defiance in 1955 sparked the Montgomery Bus Boycott.

The boycott, which lasted over a year, faced significant challenges, including financial strain, legal battles, and threats of violence. Yet, the clarity of purpose that drove the civil rights movement—the unwavering belief in equality and justice—sustained the momentum of those involved. This clarity transformed individual resolve into collective action, ultimately leading to significant progress in the fight against segregation.

For individuals, the same principle applies. Whether pursuing a personal goal or navigating a professional challenge, maintaining a clear sense of purpose provides the strength to push through adversity. Reflection, journaling, or revisiting your vision statement can help reconnect you with the deeper meaning behind your efforts.

Resilience Through Adaptation

Sustaining momentum also requires adaptability. Rigidity in the face of setbacks often leads to frustration and burnout, while flexibility allows you to pivot and find alternative paths to your goal. This adaptability is akin to the concept of "antifragility," introduced by Nassim Nicholas Taleb, which describes systems that grow stronger through stress and disruption.

Consider the story of Japanese car manufacturer Toyota in the aftermath of World War II. Facing resource shortages and economic devastation, Toyota developed the "Toyota Production System," a groundbreaking approach to manufacturing that emphasized efficiency and continuous improvement. This system, born out of necessity, not only sustained the company through difficult times but also revolutionized the automotive industry.

On a personal level, embracing adaptability might involve revising timelines, exploring new strategies, or seeking additional support. For example, an entrepreneur facing funding challenges might pivot to a leaner business model or explore alternative revenue streams. This willingness to adapt ensures that momentum is not lost but redirected.

The Role of Reflection and Celebration

Reflection is a powerful tool for sustaining momentum. Taking time to assess progress, acknowledge achievements, and identify areas for improvement provides valuable insights that keep efforts aligned with your vision. Reflection also serves as a reminder of how far you've come, reinforcing confidence and motivation.

Celebrating milestones, no matter how small, is equally important. Achievements, whether completing a project, reaching a fitness goal, or resolving a conflict, deserve recognition. These moments of celebration not only boost morale but also reinforce the behaviors and habits that drive success.

For instance, a team working on a long-term project might hold regular check-ins to celebrate progress and recalibrate goals. This practice keeps the team motivated and aligned, fostering a sense of shared purpose and camaraderie.

Drawing Inspiration from Others

Stories of resilience and sustained momentum can serve as powerful sources of inspiration. One such story is that of Helen Keller, who overcame the profound challenges of being blind and deaf to become an influential author, activist, and speaker. Keller's achievements were driven by her unyielding determination and the support of her teacher, Anne Sullivan, who helped her develop the tools to communicate and learn.

Keller's journey illustrates the interplay between personal resilience and external support in sustaining momentum. By surrounding yourself with individuals who believe in your vision and share your commitment, you create a network of encouragement that helps you navigate challenges.

Practical Strategies for Sustaining Momentum

Several practical strategies can help maintain momentum during setbacks:

- **Break Goals into Smaller Steps**: Tackling a large goal can feel overwhelming, particularly when progress stalls. Breaking it into smaller, manageable steps creates a sense of accomplishment and forward motion.

- **Develop Resilient Habits**: Habits such as regular exercise, mindfulness, and time management create a stable foundation that supports consistent progress. These habits serve as anchors during periods of uncertainty.

- **Seek Feedback and Support**: Engaging with mentors, peers, or coaches provides fresh perspectives and constructive feedback. These interactions can reignite motivation and offer solutions to challenges.

Sustaining Momentum as a Way of Life

Ultimately, sustaining momentum is not about avoiding challenges but about building the capacity to move through them with purpose and resilience. It requires a mindset that embraces growth, celebrates progress, and remains steadfast in the face of uncertainty.

As the philosopher Friedrich Nietzsche observed, *"He who has a why to live for can bear almost any how."* By anchoring your efforts in clarity and purpose, you transform momentum from a fleeting force into a lasting foundation for success.

CHAPTER 6: THE ROLE OF CHAOS – FINDING MEANING IN DISORDER

Chaos as a Catalyst for Growth

Chaos is often perceived as a force of destruction—a state of disorder that disrupts routines, shatters plans, and creates uncertainty. Yet, chaos also holds the potential for profound transformation. Like the churning of a storm that clears the air, chaos can catalyze growth, clarity, and renewal. It forces us to confront the unknown, to adapt, and to reevaluate our priorities. Through this lens, chaos becomes not a threat but an opportunity—an integral part of the journey toward meaning and purpose.

The Nature of Chaos and Growth

Chaos is an inherent part of existence. From the unpredictable patterns of nature to the sudden shifts in human history, disorder is woven into the fabric of life. The ancient Greeks recognized this duality, personifying chaos not as a destructive force but as the primal void from which all creation emerged. In Greek mythology, Chaos was the origin of the cosmos, a state of boundless potential that gave birth to order and structure.

This perspective resonates with modern ideas

of growth and transformation. Chaos often dismantles the familiar, compelling us to adapt and innovate. As the psychologist Carl Jung observed, *"In all chaos, there is a cosmos; in all disorder, a secret order."* Chaos challenges us to move beyond comfort zones, sparking creativity and resilience.

Historical Examples of Chaos as a Catalyst

History provides countless examples of chaos serving as a crucible for growth. Consider the Renaissance, a period of extraordinary cultural, scientific, and intellectual advancement born from the chaos of the Middle Ages. The collapse of feudal structures, devastating plagues, and political upheaval created a fertile ground for new ideas and perspectives to flourish. Visionaries like Leonardo da Vinci, Michelangelo, and Galileo thrived in this environment, redefining art, science, and human potential.

In more recent history, the Great Depression of the 1930s serves as another example. This period of economic turmoil brought immense hardship, but it also spurred transformative changes. Governments implemented groundbreaking social programs, industries adapted to shifting demands, and individuals found innovative ways to survive and thrive. The chaos of the Depression laid the foundation for resilience and progress, shaping modern economies and societies.

On a personal level, chaos often forces individuals to confront challenges that lead to self-discovery and growth. Think of an entrepreneur whose business faces sudden adversity, prompting them to pivot and create a new, more impactful venture. Or consider someone navigating a major life transition, such as a career change or the end of a relationship. These periods of upheaval, while painful, often spark profound personal growth and clarity about what truly matters.

Philosophical Reflections on Chaos

Philosophers throughout history have grappled with the role of chaos in human experience. Friedrich Nietzsche, for instance, embraced the transformative power of chaos, famously stating, *"One must still have chaos in oneself to be able to give birth to a dancing star."* For Nietzsche, chaos was not a state to be feared but a source of creative energy and possibility.

The Stoics, too, offered insights into navigating chaos. They taught that while we cannot control external events, we can control our responses. This philosophy encourages reframing chaos as an opportunity to practice resilience and adaptability. Marcus Aurelius, the Roman emperor and Stoic philosopher, wrote in his *Meditations*: *"You have power over your mind—not outside events. Realize this, and you will find strength."*

These reflections underscore an important truth: chaos is not inherently negative. It is our perception of and response to chaos that determines its impact. By shifting our perspective, we can transform chaos into a catalyst for growth.

The Role of Clarity in Chaos

Clarity emerges as both a product and a guide through chaos. When faced with disorder, clarity helps us identify what is essential, stripping away distractions and focusing on what truly matters. Chaos has a way of revealing priorities, forcing us to reassess our values and goals.

This dynamic is evident in the stories of leaders who thrived amidst turmoil. Take Abraham Lincoln, who led the United States during the Civil War. The chaos of the conflict tested his resolve and leadership, yet Lincoln's clarity of purpose—preserving the Union and abolishing slavery—provided a steady compass. His ability to navigate the disorder of war with focus and determination solidified his legacy as one of history's greatest leaders.

Clarity does not eliminate chaos, but it provides a framework for navigating it. It helps us make sense of the disorder, enabling us to act with intention and purpose even in the face of uncertainty.

Practical Applications: Embracing Chaos for Growth

To harness chaos as a catalyst for growth, we must first shift our mindset. Instead of resisting or fearing chaos, we can embrace it as an opportunity for transformation. This requires cultivating curiosity, adaptability, and resilience.

One practical approach is to view chaos as a learning experience. When faced with disruption, ask:

- *What can I learn from this situation?*

- *How might this challenge help me grow?*

- *What opportunities does this chaos reveal?*

Another strategy is to focus on small, actionable steps. Chaos often feels overwhelming because of its complexity and scale. By breaking challenges into manageable tasks, we regain a sense of control and momentum. For example, during a career transition, instead of fixating on the uncertainty of the future, focus on updating your resume, networking, or acquiring new skills.

Reflection is also key. Periods of chaos often provide powerful insights, but only if we take the time to process them. Journaling, meditation, or discussing experiences with a trusted mentor can help uncover the lessons hidden within the disorder.

Finally, surround yourself with supportive networks. Chaos can be isolating, but leaning on others—whether friends, family, or professional mentors—provides strength and perspective. Collaborative problem-solving often reveals solutions that might not be apparent in isolation.

Conclusion: Finding Growth in Disorder

Chaos, while challenging, is a natural and necessary part of life. It disrupts the status quo, forcing us to confront new realities and adapt to changing circumstances. By reframing chaos as a catalyst for growth, we unlock its transformative potential, discovering clarity, purpose, and resilience along the way.

As the poet Rainer Maria Rilke wrote, *"Let everything happen to you: beauty and terror. Just keep going. No feeling is final."* Chaos is not the end; it is a beginning—a powerful force that propels us toward growth, meaning, and a deeper understanding of ourselves and the world.

Navigating Uncertainty with Perspective

Uncertainty is an inevitable part of life, but

it often feels like an unwelcome guest. It disrupts plans, shakes confidence, and forces us to confront the unknown. Yet, how we navigate uncertainty determines whether it becomes a source of anxiety or an opportunity for growth. Perspective—the ability to step back, reframe, and see the bigger picture—is the compass that guides us through uncharted territory. By cultivating adaptability and foresight, we can find stability amid chaos and transform uncertainty into clarity.

The Nature of Uncertainty

Uncertainty is not merely a modern phenomenon; it has been a defining feature of the human experience throughout history. From the unpredictability of nature to the complexities of social and political change, uncertainty challenges our need for control and stability.

Philosophers and thinkers have long grappled with this reality. The Stoics, for example, emphasized the importance of accepting what lies beyond our control. Epictetus wrote, *"It's not what happens to you, but how you react to it that matters."* This mindset encourages a shift from resisting uncertainty to embracing it as an inherent part of life.

In today's fast-paced world, uncertainty often takes the form of rapid technological changes, economic fluctuations, or personal transitions. While these challenges may feel overwhelming, they also offer opportunities to develop resilience, creativity, and new perspectives.

Adaptability: The Key to Navigating Change

Adaptability is the cornerstone of navigating uncertainty. It is the ability to adjust to new circumstances, rethink assumptions, and approach challenges with a flexible mindset. Adaptable individuals and societies not only survive but often thrive in the face of change.

One powerful example is Charles Darwin's theory of evolution, which emphasizes that it is not the strongest or the most intelligent species that survive, but those most adaptable to change. This principle applies not only to biology but also to personal and professional growth.

During the COVID-19 pandemic, adaptability

became a defining trait of resilience. Businesses that pivoted quickly—shifting to remote work, rethinking supply chains, or launching new products—weathered the storm more effectively than those resistant to change. On a personal level, individuals who embraced new routines, learned digital skills, or found creative ways to stay connected demonstrated the power of adaptability in uncertain times.

Foresight: Anticipating the Unseen

While adaptability focuses on responding to change, foresight involves anticipating it. Foresight does not require predicting the future with precision but rather cultivating the ability to identify patterns, imagine possibilities, and prepare for a range of outcomes.

One historical example of foresight is the work of Florence Nightingale during the Crimean War. Faced with appalling conditions in military hospitals, Nightingale used her knowledge of sanitation and statistics to anticipate the impact of poor hygiene on soldier mortality. Her reforms, informed by foresight and grounded in data, not only saved countless lives but also transformed healthcare practices worldwide.

Foresight can also be seen in the realm of business and innovation. Visionary leaders like Steve Jobs demonstrated an ability to anticipate technological trends and consumer needs, creating products that shaped entire industries. Jobs's foresight was not about guessing the future but about deeply understanding human behavior, identifying gaps, and imagining possibilities.

Cultivating foresight involves staying informed, asking "what if" questions, and considering long-term implications. For example, when faced with a career decision, foresight might involve exploring how different industries are evolving, seeking mentors, and envisioning the skills that will be most valuable in the coming years.

Practical Tools for Staying Grounded

Navigating uncertainty requires not only adaptability and foresight but also practical tools for staying grounded. One such tool is mindfulness, the practice of anchoring oneself in the present moment. Mindfulness reduces the mental noise of "what ifs," allowing us to focus on what we can control here and now.

Consider a professional facing an unexpected job loss. Mindfulness might involve acknowledging the fear and uncertainty of the situation while redirecting attention to immediate steps: updating a resume, networking, or identifying transferable skills. This focus on the present creates a sense of agency, reducing the overwhelm of uncertainty.

Another powerful tool is reframing—shifting how we perceive a situation to uncover its potential benefits. For example, a person navigating a difficult relocation might initially view it as a loss of stability. By reframing, they might see it as an opportunity to explore a new environment, meet diverse people, and grow in unexpected ways.

Reflection also plays a crucial role in navigating uncertainty. Regularly pausing to assess your thoughts, emotions, and progress provides clarity and perspective. Journaling, meditation, or discussing challenges with a trusted mentor can help uncover insights and guide decisions.

Historical Perspectives on Navigating Uncertainty

History offers valuable lessons on how individuals and societies have navigated uncertainty with perspective. During the Great Depression, Franklin D. Roosevelt's leadership exemplified the power of clear communication and collective purpose. His "fireside chats" provided reassurance and guidance, helping Americans focus on actionable solutions rather than succumbing to despair.

On a personal level, figures like Viktor Frankl, a Holocaust survivor and psychiatrist, demonstrated extraordinary resilience amid profound uncertainty. In his book, *Man's Search for Meaning*, Frankl argued that even in the most chaotic circumstances, individuals can find purpose by focusing on what they can control—their attitudes and actions.

These examples highlight the transformative power of perspective. By shifting focus from the uncontrollable to the actionable, we not only navigate uncertainty but also emerge stronger and more purposeful.

The Interplay Between Perspective and Growth

Uncertainty often serves as a crucible for growth. It forces us to question assumptions, explore new paths, and develop resilience. The philosopher Søren Kierkegaard described this dynamic as the "dizziness of freedom"—the unsettling yet liberating experience of facing the unknown.

For instance, consider an artist experiencing a creative block. While uncertainty about their next project might feel paralyzing, it also creates space for experimentation and discovery. By exploring new mediums, seeking inspiration from unexpected sources, or collaborating with others, the artist transforms uncertainty into a catalyst for innovation.

Conclusion: Embracing Uncertainty with Perspective

Navigating uncertainty is not about eliminating doubt but about finding clarity and purpose within it. By cultivating adaptability, foresight, and practical tools for staying grounded, we transform uncertainty from a source of fear into an opportunity for growth.

As the poet Rumi wrote, *"Try not to resist the changes that come your way. Instead, let life live through you. And do not worry that your life is turning upside down. How do you know that the side you are used to is better than the one to come?"* With perspective, uncertainty becomes not an obstacle but a doorway to new possibilities.

Lessons from Historical Disruptions

History is a chronicle of disruptions—wars, revolutions, pandemics, and economic upheavals—that have challenged the foundations of societies. Yet, within these turbulent periods lie profound lessons about resilience, adaptation, and transformation. By examining how individuals and communities have navigated historical disruptions, we uncover timeless principles for thriving amidst chaos. These stories reveal that even in the darkest times, perspective and purpose can illuminate a path forward.

The Black Death and the Dawn of a New Era

One of history's most devastating disruptions was the Black Death, which swept through Europe in the 14th century, claiming millions of lives. The pandemic shattered social structures, disrupted economies, and spread fear and uncertainty across the continent. Yet, in its aftermath, the Black Death catalyzed significant social, cultural, and economic changes.

The labor shortages caused by the pandemic shifted power dynamics, as peasants and workers gained leverage to demand better wages and conditions. This redistribution of power laid the groundwork for the decline of feudalism and the emergence of a more dynamic economy. Culturally, the upheaval inspired introspection and creativity, fueling the Renaissance—a period of unparalleled artistic and intellectual growth.

Figures like Leonardo da Vinci and Michelangelo flourished during this transformative era, their works reflecting a renewed focus on human potential and perspective. The resilience and ingenuity that emerged from the chaos of the Black Death remind us that disruption, while painful, can also be a powerful force for renewal.

The American Civil Rights Movement: Transforming Injustice into Progress

The civil rights movement in the United States is another powerful example of thriving amidst disruption. This era, marked by widespread racial injustice and social unrest, demanded extraordinary courage and vision from its leaders. Figures like Martin Luther King Jr. and Rosa Parks exemplified the ability to harness chaos for a higher purpose, transforming division into a catalyst for change.

King's leadership during the Montgomery Bus Boycott and the March on Washington demonstrated the power of nonviolent resistance to challenge entrenched systems of oppression. His ability to articulate a clear vision of equality and justice galvanized a movement that reshaped the social fabric of the United States.

The disruptions of the civil rights era highlight the importance of perspective in navigating chaos. By reframing injustice as an opportunity to advance human rights, leaders and activists found the strength to persevere and create lasting change. Their stories remind us that even in the face of systemic challenges, clarity of purpose can inspire transformative progress.

World War II: Innovation Born of Necessity

World War II was a period of unprecedented global disruption, characterized by widespread destruction, loss, and uncertainty. Yet, it also spurred remarkable innovations that reshaped the modern world.

The Manhattan Project, for example, led to the development of nuclear technology, which, despite its destructive potential, also paved the way for advancements in energy and medicine. The war also accelerated the development of radar, jet engines, and computing technology—innovations that continue to influence modern life.

On the home front, individuals and communities adapted to wartime shortages by embracing resourcefulness and solidarity. Victory gardens, rationing, and community support networks demonstrated the power of collective resilience in overcoming adversity.

Figures like Winston Churchill epitomized leadership during chaos. Churchill's unwavering resolve and ability to rally the British people during the Blitz inspired hope and unity in the face of overwhelming challenges. His perspective—that the hardships of war were a necessary prelude to freedom and peace—underscored the importance of maintaining a clear vision during disruption.

The Great Recession: Lessons in Adaptation and Resilience

In more recent history, the Great Recession of 2008 serves as a poignant example of disruption and recovery. The global financial crisis, triggered by the collapse of major financial institutions, caused widespread unemployment, foreclosures, and economic instability. Yet, it also prompted significant reforms and innovations in industries ranging from finance to technology.

Entrepreneurs who embraced the chaos of the recession found opportunities to disrupt traditional models and create new markets. Companies like Airbnb and Uber, both founded during the recession, exemplify the ability to adapt and innovate in challenging times. By reimagining how people interact with resources like housing and transportation, these startups not only survived the economic downturn but also transformed entire industries.

For individuals, the recession underscored the importance of adaptability and foresight. Many workers pivoted to new careers, pursued further education, or embraced the gig economy to navigate the shifting landscape. These stories of resilience highlight the potential for personal growth and reinvention during periods of disruption.

Insights from Historical Disruptions

Across these examples, several recurring themes emerge:

- **Clarity of Purpose**: Leaders and innovators who thrived during disruptions maintained a clear sense of their goals and values. This clarity provided a guiding light, even in the midst of chaos.

- **Adaptability**: The ability to pivot, experiment, and embrace new approaches was essential for navigating uncertainty. Those who were willing to let go of rigid plans and explore alternative paths found opportunities for growth.

- **Community and Collaboration**: Disruptions often highlight the importance of collective action. Whether through social movements, wartime solidarity, or grassroots initiatives, collaboration amplified resilience and impact.

- **Perspective**: Reframing challenges as opportunities allowed individuals and societies to find meaning and growth in disorder. This shift in perspective transformed adversity into a catalyst for progress.

Applying These Lessons Today

The lessons of historical disruptions are as relevant today as ever. In a world characterized by rapid change and global challenges, the ability to navigate chaos with perspective and purpose is crucial. Whether facing personal setbacks, professional transitions, or societal upheaval, we can draw on these stories to guide our own journeys.

By cultivating clarity, adaptability, and a sense of shared purpose, we not only survive disruption but also emerge stronger and more intentional. As history shows, chaos is not an endpoint—it is a beginning, a powerful force that shapes the next chapter of growth and transformation.

Turning Disorder into Opportunity

Disorder, by its nature, disrupts the status quo and forces us to confront new realities. While it can be unsettling, it also holds immense potential. Disorder shakes loose rigid patterns, dismantles outdated systems, and creates space for innovation, growth, and renewal. The key to turning disorder into opportunity lies in how we perceive and respond to it. By cultivating clarity, staying adaptable, and embracing a mindset of curiosity and possibility, we can transform chaos into a powerful driver of personal and collective progress.

Reframing Chaos as Opportunity

The first step in harnessing the potential of disorder is reframing how we view it. Instead of seeing chaos as a threat, we can choose to see it as a catalyst—a force that breaks down barriers and opens up new paths. This shift in perspective requires us to focus on possibility rather than loss, on creation rather than destruction.

Consider the story of J.K. Rowling, who penned the *Harry Potter* series. Before achieving global success, Rowling faced significant personal and financial hardships. She described herself as being at "rock bottom" after a divorce and while raising her daughter as a single mother. Yet, she credited this period of intense disorder with giving her the clarity to focus on her passion for writing. By reframing her circumstances as an opportunity to rebuild, Rowling channeled her energy into creating a story that would captivate millions.

Her journey highlights an important truth: the moments when everything seems to fall apart can also be the moments when we discover our deepest potential. Disorder forces us to reassess, strip away what no longer serves us, and commit to what truly matters.

Practical Steps for Harnessing Disorder

While reframing chaos is essential, it must be paired with actionable steps to translate vision into results. One effective approach is to focus on small, deliberate actions that build momentum. Chaos often feels overwhelming because it obscures the path forward. Breaking challenges into manageable steps restores a sense of control and direction.

For example, imagine an individual whose career has been disrupted by layoffs. Instead of fixating on the uncertainty of the job market, they might take small but significant actions: updating their resume, reaching out to professional networks, or learning a new skill. Each step reinforces their agency, creating a foundation for growth.

Another strategy is to identify opportunities hidden within challenges. During the COVID-19 pandemic, many businesses adapted to the disruption by embracing digital transformation. Restaurants pivoted to online delivery models, fitness trainers offered virtual classes, and educators developed innovative approaches to remote learning. These adaptations not only addressed immediate challenges but also created new revenue streams and long-term possibilities.

Embracing a Growth Mindset

A growth mindset—the belief that abilities and intelligence can be developed through effort and perseverance—is essential for turning disorder into opportunity. Coined by psychologist Carol Dweck, this mindset encourages us to view challenges as opportunities for learning and improvement.

Take the example of Thomas Edison, who famously said, *"I have not failed. I've just found 10,000 ways that won't work."* Edison's approach to experimentation exemplifies the growth mindset. Each setback was not a failure but a step closer to innovation. This perspective not only sustained his momentum but also enabled him to achieve groundbreaking success.

Cultivating a growth mindset involves embracing curiosity, seeking feedback, and reframing setbacks as valuable learning experiences. For instance, a student struggling with a challenging subject might focus on the skills they are developing—resilience, problem-solving, and adaptability—rather than fixating on immediate results. This shift in perspective transforms obstacles into stepping stones.

Learning from Real-Life Case Studies

The stories of individuals and organizations that have thrived amidst disorder provide valuable insights into how to harness chaos effectively.

One compelling case is that of Airbnb, which was founded during the 2008 financial crisis. Facing significant economic uncertainty, the company's founders identified a need for affordable travel options and reimagined the concept of hospitality. By leveraging underutilized resources—people's homes—Airbnb disrupted the traditional hotel industry and created a global platform for shared experiences.

Their success illustrates the power of aligning solutions with emerging needs. By paying attention to shifts in the market and adapting their vision accordingly, the founders turned a moment of economic disorder into an opportunity for innovation.

The Role of Support and Collaboration

Navigating disorder is rarely a solitary endeavor. Support networks—friends, family, mentors, and communities—play a crucial role in providing perspective, encouragement, and resources. Collaboration amplifies individual efforts, transforming isolated challenges into shared opportunities.

One example of this dynamic is the rise of mutual aid networks during times of crisis. In the aftermath of natural disasters or economic downturns, communities often come together to share resources, skills, and support. These grassroots efforts not only address immediate needs but also strengthen social bonds and foster resilience.

For individuals, seeking collaboration might involve joining professional associations, participating in online forums, or forming study groups. These connections provide fresh perspectives, spark creative ideas, and create a sense of shared purpose.

Reflection and Clarity Amid Disorder

Turning disorder into opportunity requires regular reflection to ensure that actions align with long-term goals. Taking time to pause, assess progress, and recalibrate strategies allows us to stay focused and intentional.

Reflection might involve journaling, meditating, or engaging in deep conversations with trusted confidants. These practices provide clarity, helping us identify what is working, what needs adjustment, and what opportunities are emerging. For instance, an entrepreneur navigating a competitive market might reflect on customer feedback to refine their offerings, ensuring they remain relevant and valuable.

The Transformative Potential of Disorder

Ultimately, disorder is not an endpoint but a starting point—a powerful force that drives growth, innovation, and self-discovery. By embracing chaos with curiosity, adaptability, and resilience, we unlock its transformative potential.

As the author Anaïs Nin wrote, *"Life shrinks or expands in proportion to one's courage."* Courageously confronting disorder allows us to expand our horizons, explore new possibilities, and create meaning from uncertainty. Disorder challenges us to rethink, reimagine, and rebuild, paving the way for a brighter and more purposeful future.

CHAPTER 7: THE INNER WORLD – GAINING PERSPECTIVE ON YOURSELF

The Journey of Self-Awareness

Self-awareness is the cornerstone of gaining perspective. It is the lens through which we understand our thoughts, emotions, and behaviors, allowing us to navigate life with clarity and intentionality. Without self-awareness, we risk being driven by unconscious patterns, reactive emotions, and external influences, losing sight of who we are and what truly matters. Developing self-awareness is not a one-time achievement but a continuous journey—a process of peeling back layers to uncover our authentic selves.

Understanding the Foundation of Self-Awareness

At its core, self-awareness is the ability to observe ourselves objectively. It involves recognizing our strengths and weaknesses, understanding our values and motivations, and being attuned to how we affect others. This understanding forms the bedrock of emotional intelligence—a concept popularized by psychologist Daniel Goleman, who identified self-awareness as one of its five critical components.

Emotional intelligence, or EQ, extends beyond managing emotions; it encompasses the ability to empathize, build relationships, and make thoughtful decisions. Self-awareness is the starting point, enabling us to regulate our emotions, respond rather than react, and align our actions with our intentions.

Consider the example of Mahatma Gandhi, a leader whose profound self-awareness shaped his approach to social change. Gandhi's philosophy of nonviolence was not merely a political strategy but an extension of his inner clarity and discipline. Through practices like fasting and meditation, Gandhi cultivated a deep understanding of his values and emotions, allowing him to lead with authenticity and inspire millions. His journey reminds us that self-awareness is not only a personal endeavor but also a force for transformation in the world.

The Role of Self-Awareness in Personal Growth

Self-awareness serves as a compass for personal growth. It helps us identify areas where we can improve while celebrating our unique strengths. Without this clarity, growth becomes aimless—a series of actions disconnected from a deeper sense of purpose.

The process of self-awareness often begins with asking difficult questions:

- *What motivates my choices?*

- *How do my actions align with my values?*

- *What patterns in my behavior hold me back?*

These questions require courage and honesty, as they often reveal uncomfortable truths. Yet, it is in confronting these truths that we open the door to meaningful change. For example, an individual struggling with procrastination might uncover that their habit stems not from laziness but from fear of failure. This insight shifts the focus from blame to understanding, paving the way for constructive solutions.

Philosopher Socrates famously declared, *"The unexamined life is not worth living."* This assertion underscores the importance of self-awareness as a pathway to authenticity and fulfillment. When we examine our lives with curiosity and compassion, we gain the perspective needed to make conscious choices and pursue what truly matters.

Historical Lessons in Self-Awareness

Throughout history, figures who achieved great impact often demonstrated a profound understanding of themselves. Leonardo da Vinci, for instance, kept detailed journals in which he documented his thoughts, observations, and aspirations. These journals reveal not only his genius but also his commitment to introspection—a practice that allowed him to explore his curiosity and refine his ideas.

Similarly, Eleanor Roosevelt's journey of self-awareness shaped her evolution as a leader and advocate for human rights. In her autobiography, Roosevelt reflected on her early insecurities and how she overcame them through self-examination and service to others. Her willingness to confront her fears and limitations enabled her to grow into one of the most influential figures of her time.

These stories illustrate that self-awareness is not about achieving perfection but about embracing the ongoing process of growth. By understanding ourselves, we gain the clarity to navigate challenges, build resilience, and contribute meaningfully to the world.

Practical Applications of Self-Awareness

While the concept of self-awareness may seem abstract, its applications are both practical and transformative. One approach to developing self-awareness is mindfulness—the practice of observing our thoughts and emotions without judgment. Mindfulness cultivates a state of presence, allowing us to identify patterns and triggers that influence our behavior.

Imagine an individual who frequently experiences conflict in relationships. Through mindfulness, they might notice a tendency to react defensively when feeling criticized. This awareness creates space for a new response—one rooted in understanding rather than reactivity. Over time, this shift strengthens relationships and fosters emotional well-being.

Another powerful tool is journaling. Writing about our experiences, thoughts, and feelings provides a structured way to explore our inner world. Journaling not only clarifies emotions but also uncovers recurring themes and insights that guide decision-making. For example, an entrepreneur reflecting on their daily challenges might identify that their stress stems from over-committing. This realization empowers them to set boundaries and prioritize effectively.

Feedback from trusted individuals also enhances self-awareness. While introspection is invaluable, external perspectives provide insights we might overlook. Seeking feedback requires vulnerability, but it opens the door to deeper understanding and growth. For instance, a leader might ask their team for honest input on their communication style, using the feedback to refine their approach and build stronger connections.

The Interplay Between Self-Awareness and Perspective

Self-awareness and perspective are intrinsically

linked. As we deepen our understanding of ourselves, we become better equipped to understand others. This interplay enhances empathy, strengthens relationships, and broadens our worldview.

For example, consider a teacher who reflects on their own learning process—acknowledging the challenges they faced and the strategies that helped them succeed. This self-awareness enables the teacher to empathize with their students, tailoring their approach to meet diverse needs.

Similarly, self-awareness enhances our ability to navigate complex situations. By recognizing our biases and assumptions, we approach challenges with greater objectivity and clarity. This expanded perspective empowers us to find solutions that align with our values and priorities.

The Transformative Power of Self-Awareness

The journey of self-awareness is not linear or finite; it is a lifelong process of discovery and refinement. Each layer of understanding brings us closer to our authentic selves, enabling us to live with intention and purpose.

As we cultivate self-awareness, we unlock the ability to see ourselves—and the world—with greater clarity. This clarity is not only a gift to ourselves but also to those around us. When we act from a place of understanding, we inspire trust, foster connection, and contribute to a more compassionate and thoughtful world.

The journey of self-awareness, though challenging, is among the most rewarding paths we can undertake. As the poet Rumi wrote, *"The soul has been given its own ears to hear things the mind does not understand."* By listening to ourselves with curiosity and compassion, we uncover the wisdom that guides us toward growth, fulfillment, and purpose.

Tools for Introspection

Introspection is the bridge between self-awareness and transformation. It allows us to delve into our inner world, exploring the beliefs, emotions, and motivations that shape our actions. Through intentional reflection, we gain clarity about our strengths, challenges, and desires, equipping ourselves to make conscious choices and embrace growth. While introspection requires vulnerability and effort, it is a deeply empowering process, enabling us to navigate life with purpose and authenticity.

Throughout history, many have turned to introspective practices to uncover truths about themselves and the world around them. From journaling to meditation to philosophical reflection, these tools not only illuminate our inner landscapes but also provide practical strategies for understanding and evolving.

The Power of Journaling

Journaling is one of the simplest yet most profound tools for introspection. By putting thoughts to paper, we externalize our inner dialogue, gaining distance and perspective on our experiences. Journaling helps us organize our thoughts, identify patterns, and process emotions in a structured and constructive way.

Consider the example of Marcus Aurelius, the Roman emperor and Stoic philosopher, whose personal journal became the timeless work *Meditations*. In his writings, Marcus reflected on his responsibilities, ethical dilemmas, and the fleeting nature of life. His journal served as a tool for self-examination and clarity, helping him navigate the complexities of leadership with wisdom and composure.

For modern readers, journaling offers similar benefits. Whether through daily gratitude entries, reflections on challenges, or freewriting, the act of journaling fosters self-awareness and emotional processing. For example, someone facing a difficult decision might use journaling to explore their fears, values, and potential outcomes, ultimately clarifying their path forward.

A practical starting point for journaling is the "three-question" method:

1. *What am I feeling right now?*

2. *What is driving this feeling?*

3. *What can I do about it?*

These questions encourage honesty and

self-compassion, transforming journaling into a practice of discovery and empowerment.

The Stillness of Meditation

Meditation is another powerful tool for introspection, offering a pathway to stillness and self-awareness. By quieting the mind and focusing on the present moment, meditation helps us observe our thoughts and emotions without judgment. This practice cultivates mindfulness — the ability to stay grounded and attentive in the here and now.

The Buddha's teachings are among the earliest examples of meditation as a means of introspection and enlightenment. Through mindfulness and contemplation, the Buddha encouraged individuals to confront their suffering, understand its origins, and cultivate inner peace. These principles, rooted in ancient wisdom, continue to resonate in modern meditation practices.

Research underscores the transformative potential of meditation. Studies have shown that regular meditation reduces stress, enhances emotional regulation, and improves focus. It also fosters a sense of self-awareness, enabling practitioners to recognize automatic patterns and respond to life's challenges with greater clarity.

For those new to meditation, starting with just a few minutes of mindful breathing each day can be impactful. Focusing on the inhale and exhale, observing thoughts as they arise without clinging to them, creates a space for self-reflection and calm. Over time, this practice deepens, revealing insights into the patterns and tendencies that shape our inner world.

The Practice of Self-Reflection

Self-reflection involves consciously examining our thoughts, behaviors, and experiences to extract meaning and insights. Unlike journaling or meditation, which often involve structured practices, self-reflection can occur spontaneously—during a quiet walk, a conversation, or a moment of solitude.

One historical figure who exemplified the power of self-reflection is Søren Kierkegaard, the Danish philosopher known as the "father of existentialism." Kierkegaard's writings emphasize the importance of examining one's life to uncover its true essence. In his work *The Sickness Unto Death*, he explores the concept of authenticity, urging individuals to confront their inner contradictions and align their actions with their deepest truths.

Self-reflection often begins with questions that challenge assumptions and encourage growth. For instance:

- *Why did I react the way I did?*

- *What can I learn from this experience?*

- *How can I approach similar situations differently in the future?*

These inquiries prompt deeper understanding and accountability, transforming everyday moments into opportunities for growth.

Historical Figures and Introspection

History offers numerous examples of individuals who embraced introspection as a means of personal and professional growth. Leonardo da Vinci, the quintessential Renaissance thinker, kept meticulous notebooks documenting his observations, ideas, and questions. His habit of introspection not only fueled his creativity but also deepened his understanding of the natural world.

Similarly, Eleanor Roosevelt, First Lady of the United States and a champion of human rights, regularly reflected on her actions and beliefs. In her autobiography, Roosevelt wrote about overcoming personal insecurities through self-examination, finding strength in her vulnerabilities. Her introspective practices shaped her leadership, enabling her to advocate for social justice with empathy and conviction.

These stories illustrate that introspection is not confined to any single domain—it is a universal tool for understanding and transformation. Whether in art, politics, or personal growth, the practice of turning inward provides the clarity needed to navigate outward challenges.

Practical Strategies for Introspection

For those seeking to cultivate introspection, the key is to find a practice that resonates and commit to it consistently. Journaling, meditation, and self-reflection each offer unique benefits, and many individuals combine these methods to deepen their understanding.

A practical approach might involve setting aside time each day for introspection—whether through a morning journal entry, an evening meditation, or a reflective walk. Creating a dedicated space and routine helps anchor the practice, making it an integral part of daily life.

For those who prefer structure, guided journaling prompts or meditation apps can provide direction and support. For instance, prompts like "What am I most grateful for today?" or "What lesson did I learn from today's challenges?" encourage meaningful reflection.

The Rewards of Introspection

The journey of introspection is not always easy—it requires patience, honesty, and vulnerability. Yet, the rewards are immense. By exploring our inner world, we gain clarity about our values, motivations, and aspirations. This clarity empowers us to make intentional choices, build authentic relationships, and navigate life with confidence and purpose.

As the philosopher Laozi observed, *"Knowing others is intelligence; knowing yourself is true wisdom."* Introspection bridges the gap between these two forms of understanding, enabling us to grow not only as individuals but also as members of a larger community. By turning inward, we unlock the perspective and strength needed to thrive in an ever-changing world.

Aligning Actions with Core Values

In a world filled with distractions and competing priorities, it is easy to lose sight of what truly matters. Aligning our actions with our core values serves as a compass, guiding us toward a life of authenticity, purpose, and fulfillment. Core values are the principles that resonate most deeply with who we are—they shape our decisions, influence our relationships, and define what we consider meaningful. When our actions align with these values, we experience a sense of harmony and integrity. When they do not, we feel conflicted and adrift.

Discovering and living by our values is not a passive process; it requires reflection, intention, and courage. By clarifying what we stand for and committing to act accordingly, we bridge the gap between who we are and who we aspire to be.

The Foundation of Core Values

Core values are deeply personal, yet they often emerge from shared human experiences. Values like honesty, compassion, justice, and curiosity transcend cultural and historical boundaries, reflecting universal aspirations for a meaningful life. At the same time, our individual values are shaped by our upbringing, experiences, and inner reflections.

Consider the story of Nelson Mandela, whose unwavering commitment to justice and equality defined his life and legacy. Mandela's values were not abstract ideals but principles that guided his every action—from his resistance to apartheid to his advocacy for reconciliation and peace. Despite decades of imprisonment and immense personal sacrifice, Mandela remained steadfast in his beliefs, transforming his values into a force for global change.

His example illustrates that core values provide both clarity and strength, anchoring us in times of uncertainty and challenge. By identifying what matters most, we create a framework for making decisions that align with our authentic selves.

Clarifying Your Core Values

Clarifying core values begins with introspection—an honest exploration of what we hold dear and why. This process often involves examining pivotal moments in our lives, when we felt most fulfilled or most conflicted. These experiences reveal patterns and priorities that point toward our values.

For example, someone who feels energized by mentoring others might identify a core value of helping others grow. Similarly, an individual who feels fulfilled when creating art may value self-expression or creativity. By reflecting on these moments, we uncover the principles that bring us closer to our true selves.

Philosophers like Aristotle emphasized the importance of living in accordance with one's values as a pathway to *eudaimonia*, or human flourishing. For Aristotle, a virtuous life—one aligned with wisdom, courage, and integrity—was the highest form of fulfillment. His teachings remind us that values are not just ideals to admire but principles to embody.

Bridging the Gap Between Values and Actions

While identifying values is essential, aligning actions with those values is where transformation occurs. This alignment requires consistent effort, self-awareness, and a willingness to confront discomfort.

One practical approach is to evaluate daily choices through the lens of values. For instance, someone who values family might reflect on how their work-life balance supports or detracts from that priority. Similarly, an entrepreneur who values innovation might assess whether their business decisions foster creativity or merely replicate conventional models.

The process of alignment also involves setting boundaries and saying no to commitments that conflict with our values. This can be challenging, particularly in a world that often rewards external validation over internal integrity. Yet, by honoring our principles, we build a life that reflects our authentic selves.

A striking example of this alignment is seen in the life of Mahatma Gandhi. Gandhi's principle of *ahimsa*, or nonviolence, was not limited to his political activism but extended to every aspect of his life—from his diet to his interpersonal relationships. His unwavering commitment to this value earned him respect and credibility, enabling him to lead a movement that transformed an entire nation.

The Role of Reflection in Maintaining Alignment

Maintaining alignment between actions and values requires regular reflection. Life is dynamic, and as circumstances change, so too may the ways we express our values. Reflection provides an opportunity to reassess, recalibrate, and ensure that our actions remain true to our principles.

For instance, a professional facing a career transition might reflect on how their new role aligns with their values of purpose and growth. This introspection not only informs decisions but also fosters a deeper sense of fulfillment and direction.

Journaling, mindfulness, and conversations with trusted mentors are valuable tools for this reflective process. They create space to explore questions like:

- *Am I living in accordance with my values?*

- *What actions have reinforced or undermined my principles?*

- *How can I better align my daily choices with what matters most?*

These reflections cultivate self-awareness and accountability, ensuring that values remain a guiding force in our lives.

The Fulfillment of Living by Your Values

Aligning actions with core values leads to a profound sense of fulfillment. When we live in harmony with our principles, we experience what psychologist Carl Rogers called *congruence*—a state where our inner beliefs and outward actions are aligned. This congruence fosters authenticity, resilience, and a deep sense of purpose.

Consider the story of Jane Goodall, whose dedication to environmental conservation reflects her values of compassion, curiosity, and stewardship. Goodall's alignment of actions with values has not only advanced scientific understanding but also inspired generations to protect the natural world. Her life demonstrates that when we live by our values, we not only find personal meaning but also create a positive impact on others.

Practical Strategies for Alignment

To align actions with values, it is helpful to develop specific practices that reinforce your principles. One such practice is setting intentions at the start of each day, focusing on how you want to show up in alignment with your values. For example, if kindness is a core value, you might set the intention to approach interactions with patience and empathy.

Another strategy is to create visual reminders of your values, such as a written list, a vision board, or symbolic objects. These reminders serve as touchstones, keeping your principles front and center amidst daily distractions.

Finally, surrounding yourself with individuals who share or respect your values strengthens your commitment to living authentically. Communities of support provide encouragement, accountability, and inspiration, reinforcing the alignment between beliefs and actions.

The Transformative Power of Alignment

Aligning actions with core values is not merely a personal endeavor—it is a transformative practice that ripples outward. When we live by our principles, we inspire others to do the same, creating a culture of integrity and purpose.

As the writer Ralph Waldo Emerson observed, *"To be yourself in a world that is constantly trying to make you something else is the greatest accomplishment."* By staying true to our values, we honor our unique journey and contribute to a world that values authenticity and connection.

Living in alignment with our values is a lifelong process, one that demands reflection, intention, and courage. Yet, it is a journey well worth taking, for it leads not only to personal fulfillment but also to a life of meaning, impact, and harmony.

Overcoming Self-Deception

Self-deception is a subtle yet pervasive force that clouds our judgment, distorts our perspective, and hinders personal growth. It manifests in various forms, from justifying unhealthy habits to ignoring uncomfortable truths. At its core, self-deception is a defense mechanism—a way to shield ourselves from pain, discomfort, or the fear of inadequacy. However, the cost of maintaining these illusions is steep, as it prevents us from confronting reality and evolving into our fullest potential.

Overcoming self-deception requires courage, self-honesty, and deliberate effort. It is a process of peeling back layers of bias and blind spots to uncover the truths we may prefer to avoid. While the journey can be challenging, it is also profoundly liberating, leading to greater clarity, authenticity, and resilience.

Recognizing Blind Spots

The first step in overcoming self-deception is acknowledging that we all have blind spots—areas of our lives or behaviors that we fail to see clearly. These blind spots are often shaped by cognitive biases, past experiences, and deeply ingrained beliefs. For example, someone who struggles with perfectionism might convince themselves that their high standards are necessary for success, overlooking the toll it takes on their well-being.

Blind spots are not inherently negative; they are simply a part of being human. However, left unchecked, they can create significant barriers to growth and understanding. Recognizing their existence is a powerful act of self-awareness, one that opens the door to greater self-honesty.

Addressing Cognitive Biases

Cognitive biases — systematic errors in thinking — play a significant role in self-deception. These biases warp our perception of reality, leading us to make decisions based on incomplete or distorted information. Two common biases that contribute to self-deception are confirmation bias and the Dunning-Kruger effect.

- **Confirmation bias** occurs when we seek out information that aligns with our existing beliefs while ignoring evidence that contradicts them. For instance, an individual who believes they are a poor communicator might focus exclusively on moments of awkwardness, disregarding instances where they connect effectively with others.

- **The Dunning-Kruger effect** describes the tendency of individuals to overestimate their competence in areas where they lack knowledge. This bias can lead to misplaced confidence and an inability to recognize areas for improvement.

Overcoming these biases requires intentional effort. Practicing intellectual humility—acknowledging that we don't have all the answers—creates space for growth. Seeking diverse perspectives, inviting constructive feedback, and questioning our assumptions help counteract these biases and bring us closer to the truth.

The Role of Self-Limiting Beliefs

Self-limiting beliefs are another form of self-deception, one that constrains our potential and undermines our confidence. These beliefs often stem from past experiences, cultural influences, or internalized criticism. For example, someone who believes they are not creative might avoid pursuing artistic endeavors, despite having untapped potential.

Challenging self-limiting beliefs begins with identifying their origins. Reflecting on questions like *"Where did this belief come from?"* and *"Is it based on evidence or assumption?"* can help uncover the root of the deception. Once identified, these beliefs can be reframed into empowering narratives. For instance, replacing *"I'm not creative"* with *"Creativity is a skill I can develop through practice"* shifts the focus from limitation to possibility.

Practical Exercises for Self-Honesty

Cultivating self-honesty is essential for overcoming self-deception. While honesty with others is often emphasized, being truthful with ourselves is equally important. Here are some practical exercises to foster self-honesty and clarity:

1. **The "Mirror Test"**: Spend a few minutes each day looking in the mirror and asking yourself, *"Am I being true to myself today?"* This practice encourages accountability and creates a space for introspection.

2. **Write Your Own Eulogy**: Imagining how you want to be remembered helps clarify your values and priorities. It also highlights discrepancies between your current actions and your ideal self.

3. **Conduct a Bias Inventory**: Reflect on situations where biases may have influenced your decisions. Consider how these biases affected

your perspective and what steps you can take to counteract them in the future.

4. Seek Honest Feedback: Ask trusted friends, colleagues, or mentors for their perspective on your strengths and areas for improvement. While receiving feedback can be uncomfortable, it provides valuable insights that illuminate blind spots.

Historical Figures Who Confronted Self-Deception

History offers powerful examples of individuals who overcame self-deception to achieve profound growth and impact. One such figure is Malcolm X, whose journey of transformation exemplifies the courage to confront one's own biases and beliefs.

In his early years, Malcolm X adhered to the teachings of the Nation of Islam, which promoted racial separatism. However, during his pilgrimage to Mecca, Malcolm experienced a profound shift in perspective, witnessing the unity of people from diverse backgrounds. This revelation challenged his previous beliefs, leading him to adopt a more inclusive philosophy. His willingness to question and revise his worldview not only deepened his personal growth but also strengthened his advocacy for equality and justice.

Malcolm X's story underscores the transformative power of self-honesty. By confronting self-deception, he expanded his understanding and became a more effective leader.

The Liberating Power of Truth

Overcoming self-deception is not about achieving perfection or eliminating all biases. Rather, it is about embracing the ongoing process of seeking truth and striving for authenticity. Each step toward greater self-honesty brings freedom — freedom from the limitations of false narratives, the weight of unexamined beliefs, and the fear of confronting difficult truths.

As the philosopher Friedrich Nietzsche wrote, *"Truths are illusions we have forgotten are illusions."* Recognizing this allows us to approach self-deception with curiosity and compassion, rather than judgment. It reminds us that growth is not linear but iterative—a continuous cycle of reflection, adjustment, and renewal.

Conclusion: A Journey Worth Taking

The path to overcoming self-deception is not easy, but it is profoundly rewarding. By acknowledging blind spots, challenging biases, and embracing self-honesty, we uncover the clarity and courage needed to live authentically. This journey transforms self-deception from a barrier into a stepping stone, guiding us toward a deeper understanding of ourselves and the world.

In the words of Socrates, *"To know thyself is the beginning of wisdom."* Through the practice of self-honesty, we unlock the wisdom that lies within, empowering us to navigate life with clarity, purpose, and integrity.

CHAPTER 8: THE ART OF MASTERY – CULTIVATING A PERSPECTIVE FOR LIFE

Perspective as a Lifelong Practice

Perspective is not a static trait or a singular revelation; it is a dynamic and evolving practice that deepens as we grow. Throughout life, we encounter experiences that challenge our understanding, broaden our worldview, and refine our approach to the world. Mastery of perspective requires a commitment to continual growth—a recognition that there is always more to learn, more to explore, and more to integrate into our lives.

Just as a sculptor refines their craft over years of practice, shaping raw material into a masterpiece, we cultivate our perspective by chiseling away biases, integrating new insights, and embracing the complexities of life. This lifelong process is both humbling and empowering, reminding us that growth is an ongoing journey, not a final destination.

The Evolution of Perspective Over Time

Our perspective evolves in response to the stages of life, shaped by experiences, relationships, and personal growth. In youth, perspective is often narrow and reactive, focused on immediate needs and desires. As we age, it broadens, encompassing a deeper understanding of others, a greater appreciation for nuance, and a heightened awareness of interconnectedness.

Consider the concept of *kairos* in ancient Greek philosophy, which refers to the opportune moment for action or change. Life presents us with countless moments of *kairos* — turning points that prompt reflection and growth. These moments often arise during transitions, such as leaving home, starting a career, or facing loss. Each experience reshapes our perspective, offering lessons that guide us forward.

For example, a young professional might initially view success as a matter of individual achievement, focusing on accolades and promotions. Over time, they may come to see success as collaborative and relational, emphasizing the impact they have on their community and the legacy they leave behind. This shift in perspective reflects the natural maturation that occurs as we navigate life's challenges and opportunities.

Insights from Philosophy and Neuroscience

Philosophy and neuroscience both offer profound insights into the nature of perspective and its evolution. Philosophers like Søren Kierkegaard and Friedrich Nietzsche emphasized the transformative power of reflection and self-awareness. Kierkegaard described life as a series of stages—each requiring a leap of faith to transcend the limitations of the previous stage. This idea aligns with the concept of perspective as a dynamic practice, one that demands courage and intentionality.

From a neuroscientific perspective, our brain's ability to adapt and rewire itself—known as neuroplasticity—underscores the malleability of perspective. Studies show that engaging in reflective practices, such as mindfulness and journaling, strengthens neural pathways associated with empathy, critical thinking, and emotional regulation. These practices not only enhance our immediate perspective but also create lasting changes in how we approach life.

For instance, research conducted at Harvard University found that individuals who practice mindfulness meditation exhibit increased gray matter density in the prefrontal cortex — an area associated with self-awareness and decision-making. This finding illustrates that perspective is not merely a philosophical construct but a tangible skill that can be cultivated through deliberate effort.

The Role of Curiosity and Humility

Two qualities essential for the lifelong practice of perspective are curiosity and humility. Curiosity drives us to explore new ideas, question assumptions, and seek understanding. It opens the door to growth by encouraging us to view the world with wonder rather than judgment.

Humility, on the other hand, reminds us of our limitations. It encourages us to approach life with an open mind, recognizing that no single perspective holds the entirety of truth. Together, curiosity and humility create a fertile ground for learning and transformation.

Consider the life of Albert Einstein, who famously said, *"The important thing is not to stop questioning. Curiosity has its own reason for ex-*

isting." Einstein's relentless curiosity led to groundbreaking discoveries, while his humility allowed him to acknowledge the vastness of what remained unknown. His example underscores the interplay between curiosity and humility in cultivating a rich and evolving perspective.

Practical Strategies for Lifelong Growth

While the concept of perspective as a lifelong practice is inspiring, its application requires deliberate effort. One practical strategy is to adopt a mindset of "beginner's mind," a principle from Zen Buddhism that encourages approaching each moment as if encountering it for the first time. This mindset fosters openness and prevents the rigidity that comes with familiarity.

For example, a seasoned teacher might approach a new class with the curiosity and enthusiasm of their first year, allowing them to connect with students in fresh and meaningful ways. Similarly, an individual navigating a familiar challenge can embrace a beginner's mind to uncover new solutions and insights.

Another strategy is to actively seek diverse perspectives. Engaging with people from different backgrounds, cultures, and disciplines broadens our understanding and challenges our assumptions. Whether through travel, reading, or conversations, exposure to diverse viewpoints enriches our worldview and fosters empathy.

Reflection is also a cornerstone of lifelong growth. Setting aside time to review experiences, celebrate progress, and identify areas for improvement creates a cycle of continuous learning. This practice can be as simple as journaling at the end of each day or engaging in deep conversations with trusted mentors.

The Interconnectedness of Growth and Contribution

As our perspective evolves, so does our ability to contribute meaningfully to others. Perspective is not an isolated pursuit; it is a force that shapes how we interact with the world. By cultivating clarity and understanding, we inspire and uplift those around us, creating a ripple effect of growth and transformation.

Take, for instance, the legacy of Maya Angelou, whose rich and nuanced perspective on life informed her work as a writer, activist, and mentor. Angelou's willingness to reflect on her own experiences, confront injustices, and share her wisdom empowered countless individuals to find their own voice. Her life illustrates that the practice of perspective is not only a personal journey but also a gift to others.

Conclusion: Embracing the Practice

Perspective is not something we acquire once and for all; it is a practice that unfolds over a lifetime. Each moment, each challenge, and each insight adds depth and richness to our understanding, shaping us into more compassionate, resilient, and purposeful individuals.

By approaching perspective as a dynamic and evolving practice, we honor the complexity of life and our capacity for growth. We embrace the humility to learn, the curiosity to explore, and the courage to change. And in doing so, we cultivate a perspective that not only serves us but also inspires and uplifts the world.

As the poet Rainer Maria Rilke wrote, *"Be patient toward all that is unsolved in your heart and try to love the questions themselves."* Through the practice of perspective, we learn to live with the questions, finding clarity and meaning along the way.

Integrating Lessons into Daily Life

Perspective, no matter how profound, holds its true value in action. Insights gleaned from self-awareness, reflection, and understanding are transformative only when applied to the complexities of everyday life. By integrating clarity and perspective into our routines, we navigate challenges with greater wisdom, engage with others more compassionately, and approach decisions with intentionality. The key lies in transforming abstract lessons into tangible practices—small, consistent actions that align with our values and enhance our experience of the world.

Bringing Clarity to Everyday Decisions

Daily life is filled with moments that demand decisions, from the seemingly trivial to the deeply significant. Perspective offers a way to approach these moments with intention rather than reaction. By taking a step back to assess the bigger picture, we reduce the influence of impulsive emotions or external pressures and ensure our choices align with our goals and values.

Consider the example of an overwhelmed professional juggling multiple responsibilities. Without perspective, they might default to reactive decision-making, addressing the loudest demands while neglecting long-term priorities. By pausing to reflect—asking questions like *"What matters most right now?"* or *"Does this align with my values and goals?"*—they gain clarity and focus, enabling them to prioritize effectively and act with purpose.

Historical figures often exemplify this practice. During the Cuban Missile Crisis, President John F. Kennedy demonstrated the power of clarity in high-stakes decision-making. Faced with immense pressure and the risk of nuclear war, Kennedy and his advisors took deliberate steps to analyze the situation from multiple perspectives. By prioritizing calm reflection over reactive action, they found a peaceful resolution to one of the most dangerous moments in modern history. This example underscores the value of integrating clarity into decision-making processes, even under intense pressure.

Practicing Mindfulness in Daily Interactions

Perspective is not only about decision-making but also about how we engage with others. Practicing mindfulness in our interactions enhances empathy, reduces misunderstandings, and fosters meaningful connections. This means being fully present during conversations, listening without judgment, and seeking to understand before responding.

For example, consider a parent navigating a challenging moment with their child. Without mindfulness, frustration might lead to reactive behavior, escalating tension. With perspective, the parent can pause to recognize their own emotions, empathize with the child's experience, and respond constructively. This shift transforms a moment of conflict into an opportunity for connection and growth.

Philosophical traditions like Stoicism emphasize the importance of mindfulness in relationships. Marcus Aurelius, in his *Meditations*, reflects on the value of approaching others with patience and understanding, even when faced with challenging behavior. His writings remind us that perspective allows us to see beyond immediate frustrations and engage with others from a place of compassion.

Reframing Challenges as Opportunities

Life's challenges often feel overwhelming, but perspective allows us to reframe them as opportunities for growth. This shift in mindset requires intentional effort, but it fundamentally changes how we approach adversity. By focusing on what we can learn or achieve through difficulty, we cultivate resilience and purpose.

A practical way to apply this reframing is to ask reflective questions when facing challenges:

- *What can I learn from this experience?*

- *How does this align with my long-term goals?*

- What strengths can I develop or draw upon to navigate this?

Consider the story of Helen Keller, who, despite being blind and deaf from a young age, reframed her challenges as opportunities to advocate for disability rights and inspire others. Keller's perspective transformed her personal adversity into a force for societal change, illustrating the profound impact of reframing challenges.

For contemporary readers, this principle might apply to navigating career setbacks, health struggles, or relationship conflicts. By viewing these experiences as opportunities for growth, we find meaning and motivation, even in difficult circumstances.

Creating Space for Reflection and Integration

Reflection is essential for integrating perspective into daily life. Without time to process experiences and insights, we risk falling into habitual patterns that undermine clarity and growth. Creating intentional space for reflection allows us to evaluate our actions, celebrate progress, and identify areas for improvement.

One effective practice is to set aside time each evening to review the day. This might involve journaling about key moments, reflecting on what went well, and considering how challenges were handled. Over time, this practice deepens self-awareness and reinforces positive habits.

Another powerful tool is the "weekly reset," where individuals dedicate an hour each week to review goals, assess progress, and plan for the days ahead. This intentional pause helps align actions with values and ensures that short-term decisions contribute to long-term aspirations.

Anchoring Perspective in Rituals and Habits

Rituals and habits are powerful anchors for integrating perspective into daily life. Small, consistent practices create a foundation for clarity and intentionality, even amidst the chaos of modern living.

For instance, beginning each morning with a moment of gratitude or setting intentions for the day fosters a positive and focused mindset.

Similarly, ending the day with a brief reflection or meditation helps transition from activity to rest, promoting balance and self-awareness.

Historical examples highlight the role of rituals in cultivating perspective. Benjamin Franklin famously structured his days around a series of reflective questions, such as *"What good shall I do this day?"* and *"What good have I done today?"* These rituals reinforced his commitment to personal growth and aligned his actions with his values.

For modern readers, rituals might include practices like daily journaling, mindful breathing exercises, or dedicating time to meaningful conversations. These habits not only enhance perspective but also provide a sense of stability and purpose in an ever-changing world.

The Ripple Effect of Integrated Perspective

As we apply perspective to our own lives, its impact naturally extends outward. Clarity in decision-making, mindfulness in interactions, and resilience in challenges inspire those around us, creating a ripple effect of growth and understanding. Whether through mentorship, collaboration, or simply leading by example, the integration of perspective fosters a culture of intentionality and connection.

For example, a manager who consistently applies perspective in their leadership—balancing empathy with decisiveness—sets a tone that inspires their team to do the same. Similarly, a parent who models mindfulness and resilience teaches their children valuable life skills through their actions.

Integrating perspective into daily life is not about perfection; it is about progress. Each moment of clarity, each mindful interaction, and each reframed challenge contributes to a richer, more intentional life. By embracing these practices, we transform perspective from an abstract ideal into a lived reality—one that shapes not only our own journey but also the lives of those we touch.

Teaching Perspective to Others

Perspective is a powerful gift, and one of its most enduring legacies is the ability to share it with others. When we guide someone toward greater clarity or help them see a situation in a new light, we contribute to their growth and deepen our own understanding in the process. Perspective-sharing creates a ripple effect, influencing not only individuals but also entire communities. It is through teaching and mentorship that the seeds of clarity are planted, nurtured, and carried forward.

Whether we are parents, teachers, leaders, or friends, we all have opportunities to inspire and mentor others. By embodying perspective in our actions, engaging in meaningful conversations, and encouraging curiosity, we empower others to broaden their worldview and navigate life's complexities with wisdom and resilience.

The Ripple Effect of Perspective-Sharing

When we share perspective, its impact often extends far beyond the immediate interaction. A single insight or moment of clarity can set off a chain reaction, influencing decisions, relationships, and attitudes in ways we may never fully see.

Consider the story of Viktor Frankl, the Holocaust survivor and author of *Man's Search for Meaning*. In the harrowing environment of a concentration camp, Frankl offered his fellow prisoners a different perspective on suffering. He encouraged them to find meaning even in their darkest moments, reframing their pain as a testament to their strength and humanity. This perspective not only helped many endure unimaginable hardship but also inspired countless readers long after the war.

Frankl's example illustrates how perspective-sharing can empower others to overcome challenges and find purpose. By offering a new lens through which to view their circumstances, we help people discover their own resilience and potential.

The Art of Inspiring Clarity

Inspiring clarity in others begins with how we show up in the world. People are more likely to adopt new perspectives when they see those perspectives modeled authentically. This requires us to live with integrity, aligning our actions with our values and demonstrating the principles we hope to instill in others.

For example, a leader who prioritizes empathy and transparency creates a culture where these qualities are valued. Through their actions, they teach their team the importance of understanding others and fostering open communication. Similarly, a parent who approaches challenges with patience and curiosity teaches their child to navigate life with grace and adaptability.

Philosopher Albert Schweitzer once remarked, *"Example is not the main thing in influencing others. It is the only thing."* By embodying perspective in our own lives, we inspire others to reflect, learn, and grow.

Fostering Perspective Through Questions

One of the most effective ways to teach perspective is through questions. Rather than offering direct advice or solutions, thoughtful questions encourage others to reflect, explore, and arrive at their own insights. This approach not only respects individual autonomy but also fosters critical thinking and self-awareness.

For instance, a mentor might ask:

- *"What assumptions are you making about this situation?"*

- *"How might someone else view this differently?"*

- *"What outcome aligns most closely with your values?"*

These questions prompt deeper reflection, challenging blind spots and expanding understanding. By guiding others toward their own revelations, we empower them to develop the skills needed for lifelong growth.

Historical figures like Socrates mastered this art of questioning. Through his method of dialectical inquiry, Socrates encouraged his students to examine their beliefs, uncover contradictions, and refine their understanding. This legacy of teaching through dialogue continues to shape education and philosophy today.

Mentoring with Compassion and Curiosity

Mentorship is a profound way to share perspective, offering both guidance and support. Effective mentors balance their role as teachers with a genuine curiosity about the experiences and aspirations of those they guide. This balance creates a collaborative environment where both mentor and mentee grow.

For example, consider Maya Angelou, whose mentorship of Oprah Winfrey exemplifies the transformative power of perspective-sharing. Angelou's wisdom and encouragement helped Winfrey navigate challenges and embrace her unique voice, shaping her journey as a leader and storyteller. Through this relationship, Angelou's perspective not only influenced Winfrey but also inspired millions who have been touched by her work.

Compassion is central to this process. By approaching mentorship with empathy and understanding, we create a safe space for growth. This means listening actively, validating emotions, and offering insights that align with the individual's goals and values.

Encouraging a Growth Mindset

Teaching perspective also involves fostering a growth mindset—the belief that abilities and understanding can be developed through effort and learning. This mindset encourages resilience, adaptability, and a willingness to embrace challenges as opportunities for growth.

For instance, a teacher who emphasizes the value of mistakes as learning opportunities helps students approach difficulties with curiosity rather than fear. Similarly, a manager who celebrates progress rather than perfection inspires their team to take risks and innovate.

Carol Dweck's research on growth mindset highlights its transformative impact on individuals and organizations. By shifting focus from fixed outcomes to continuous improvement, we create an environment where perspective flourishes.

The Broader Impact of Perspective-Sharing

The effects of perspective-sharing extend far beyond individual relationships. When communities embrace clarity and intentionality, they become more collaborative, innovative, and resilient. This ripple effect is evident in movements for social change, where shared perspectives unite diverse voices around common goals.

Consider the Civil Rights Movement, where leaders like Martin Luther King Jr. inspired millions with their vision of equality and justice. Through speeches, writings, and nonviolent action, King invited others to see the world through a lens of compassion and shared humanity. His ability to articulate a clear and compelling perspective not only galvanized a generation but also reshaped societal norms.

In our own lives, we can contribute to this ripple effect by engaging in conversations that challenge assumptions, sharing stories that inspire understanding, and creating spaces for dialogue and reflection.

Conclusion: A Gift Worth Sharing

Teaching perspective is both a privilege and a responsibility. By guiding others toward clarity, we contribute to their growth and create a ripple effect that extends beyond our immediate reach. Whether through mentorship, dialogue, or simply leading by example, we inspire others to see the world—and themselves—with greater depth and understanding.

As the poet Khalil Gibran wrote, *"You give but little when you give of your possessions. It is when you give of yourself that you truly give."* Sharing perspective is one of the most meaningful ways to give of ourselves, leaving a lasting impact on the lives we touch and the world we shape.

The Legacy of a Masterful Perspective

Perspective is one of the most enduring legacies we can cultivate. It is not merely a tool for navigating life's challenges; it is a gift we leave behind, shaping how others see the world and carry forward their own journeys. The mark of a masterful perspective is its ability to transcend the individual, influencing families, communities, and even societies in ways that endure far beyond a single lifetime.

A life guided by clarity and intentionality creates ripples of understanding, compassion, and purpose. Whether through personal relationships, professional contributions, or acts of service, the legacy of perspective manifests in how we inspire, uplift, and empower others.

Perspective as a Source of Personal Fulfillment

At its core, cultivating perspective enriches our own lives. When we approach life with clarity, curiosity, and openness, we experience greater alignment between our values and actions. This congruence fosters a deep sense of fulfillment, as our choices reflect our truest selves.

Consider the life of Leonardo da Vinci, whose insatiable curiosity and multidimensional perspective left an indelible mark on art, science, and philosophy. Da Vinci's ability to see connections between seemingly disparate fields enabled him to create masterpieces like *The Last Supper* and conceptualize inventions centuries ahead of their time. His legacy demonstrates how a broad and masterful perspective fuels not only personal achievement but also contributions that inspire generations.

For contemporary readers, the lesson is clear: by committing to a perspective of continuous growth and intentionality, we create a life that feels both meaningful and impactful. Each moment of clarity becomes a building block for a legacy of purpose.

The Power of Perspective in Relationships

The legacy of perspective is perhaps most evident in our relationships. How we see and treat others profoundly shapes their experience of the world. Through empathy, understanding, and mindful communication, we foster connections that inspire growth and resilience.

A compelling example is the story of Fred Rogers, the beloved host of *Mister Rogers' Neighborhood*. Rogers' ability to connect with children and adults alike stemmed from his extraordinary perspective—a lens of kindness, patience, and deep respect for the feelings of others. His simple yet profound messages about self-worth and empathy continue to resonate, reminding us of the power of perspective to nurture love and belonging.

In our own lives, the legacy of perspective emerges in how we listen, support, and guide those around us. A parent who models patience and resilience teaches their children to approach challenges with grace. A friend who offers clarity in moments of confusion provides a foundation for growth. These everyday acts of perspective-sharing create lasting impressions, shaping the narratives of those we touch.

Perspective as a Catalyst for Societal Change

On a broader scale, a masterful perspective has the power to drive social transformation. History is filled with individuals whose clarity of vision inspired movements that changed the course of humanity. These figures remind us that perspective is not only personal but also profoundly collective—it shapes how we address shared challenges and envision a better future.

Take, for example, the legacy of Mahatma Gandhi, whose perspective on nonviolence and justice galvanized India's struggle for independence. Gandhi's unwavering commitment to his values, even in the face of immense adversity, demonstrated the transformative power of a clear and principled worldview. His teachings continue to inspire movements for peace and equality worldwide, underscoring the enduring impact of a masterful perspective.

For those seeking to leave a positive mark on society, cultivating a perspective rooted in empathy, courage, and collaboration is essential. It allows us to bridge divides, challenge injustices, and contribute to solutions that reflect our highest ideals.

Practical Steps to Create a Lasting Legacy

Leaving a legacy of perspective does not require grand gestures or historical renown. It begins with how we live each day—how we approach challenges, treat others, and align our actions with our values. Small, consistent efforts create a foundation for meaningful impact.

One way to create this legacy is by sharing our stories and lessons with others. Writing a journal, recording reflections, or simply engaging in heartfelt conversations allows us to pass on the clarity and wisdom we've gained. These acts of sharing not only benefit others but also deepen our own understanding.

Another powerful approach is mentorship. By guiding and supporting others, we amplify the impact of our perspective, creating a ripple effect that extends far beyond our immediate circle. Whether through formal mentorship programs or informal relationships, the act of sharing insights and encouragement fosters growth and resilience in others.

Inspirational Stories of Legacy

The legacies of masterful perspectives are often revealed in the lives they touch. Consider the story of Viktor Frankl, whose experiences in Nazi concentration camps led to his groundbreaking work in logotherapy. Frankl's perspective on finding meaning in suffering not only helped him survive but also inspired millions through his book *Man's Search for Meaning*. His legacy lies in the countless individuals who have drawn strength and purpose from his teachings.

Similarly, Maya Angelou's perspective on resilience and self-expression continues to resonate through her poetry, memoirs, and activism. Angelou's ability to articulate the complexities of the human experience left an enduring impact, empowering others to find their voice and embrace their identity.

These stories remind us that the legacy of perspective is not measured by fame or accolades but by the lives it influences. Each act of clarity, compassion, and courage contributes to a narrative of connection and empowerment.

Conclusion: A Legacy Worth Pursuing

The art of cultivating perspective is ultimately a gift to ourselves and others. It enriches our lives with meaning and clarity, strengthens our relationships, and contributes to the collective wisdom of humanity. By committing to this practice, we create a legacy that endures—a testament to the power of seeing the world and ourselves with depth and intention.

As we conclude this exploration of perspective, let us remember the words of poet Mary Oliver: *"Tell me, what is it you plan to do with your one wild and precious life?"* The answer lies not only in what we achieve but in how we see, share, and shape the world around us. A masterful perspective is more than a skill; it is a way of

being—one that transforms challenges into opportunities, connections into inspirations, and
lives into legacies.

CONCLUSION: A JOURNEY OF PERSPECTIVE

Throughout this book, we have explored the transformative power of perspective—the ability to see the world and ourselves with clarity, intentionality, and depth. Perspective is not merely a skill; it is a way of engaging with life that fosters growth, resilience, and fulfillment. It invites us to step beyond the confines of assumptions, biases, and limitations, enabling us to navigate challenges, build meaningful connections, and leave a lasting impact.

As we reach the conclusion of this journey, it is worth pausing to reflect on the key themes and lessons we have uncovered. Each chapter has offered insights into how perspective shapes our lives, from cultivating clarity and challenging assumptions to finding meaning in chaos and nurturing relationships. These lessons are not isolated truths but interconnected threads that weave together a richer, more intentional way of being.

The Foundation of Clarity

Perspective begins with clarity—the ability to see the world as it is, rather than as we wish or fear it to be. Clarity frees us from the distortions of bias, emotion, and misinformation, allowing us to approach decisions with wisdom and focus. It is the lens through which we discern what truly matters, aligning our actions with our values and long-term aspirations.

In cultivating clarity, we are reminded of the power of simplicity. Life often feels overwhelming, filled with competing demands and distractions. Yet clarity invites us to strip away the noise and focus on the essence of what brings meaning and purpose. This practice is not a one-time achievement but an ongoing commitment—a willingness to reflect, recalibrate, and refine our understanding as we grow.

Challenging Assumptions and Expanding Understanding

A key aspect of perspective is the courage to question our assumptions and embrace new ways of thinking. Assumptions are the invisible frameworks that shape our perceptions, often without our awareness. By challenging these frameworks, we open ourselves to growth and discovery, uncovering truths that deepen our understanding of the world.

This process is not always comfortable. It requires humility, vulnerability, and a willingness to confront the unknown. Yet the rewards are immense. When we step outside our comfort zones and engage with diverse perspectives, we expand our capacity for empathy, creativity, and insight. We learn to see the interconnectedness of life, recognizing that our own experiences are part of a broader, shared narrative.

The Resilience of Perspective in Chaos

Life is inherently unpredictable, marked by moments of chaos and uncertainty. These moments can feel disorienting, even paralyzing, as they challenge our sense of control. Yet chaos also holds the potential for transformation, offering opportunities to grow stronger, wiser, and more adaptable.

Perspective allows us to find meaning in disorder, reframing challenges as catalysts for growth. It teaches us to navigate uncertainty with grace, focusing not on what we cannot control but on how we respond. In this way, perspective becomes a source of resilience—a steady anchor amidst the shifting tides of life.

The Power of Relationships

At its heart, perspective is relational. It shapes how we connect with others, fostering empathy, understanding, and collaboration. By stepping into others' shoes, we bridge divides and build relationships grounded in mutual respect and compassion.

These connections enrich our lives and create ripples of growth and understanding. As we teach perspective to others—whether through mentorship, leadership, or simply leading by example—we amplify its impact, contributing to a culture of intentionality and connection. This ripple effect reminds us that perspective is not only personal but profoundly communal, influencing how we shape the world together.

The Legacy of Perspective

The ultimate gift of perspective is the legacy it leaves behind. A life lived with clarity, intentionality, and depth inspires others to do the same. It creates a foundation for growth and understanding that extends far beyond our individual journey.

Consider the legacies of those who have shaped history through their perspective—figures like Nelson Mandela, Maya Angelou, and Viktor Frankl. Their ability to see the world with clarity, resilience, and compassion not only transformed their own lives but also empowered countless others to find strength and meaning.

While few of us may achieve the renown of these figures, we all have the capacity to leave a meaningful legacy. Each act of clarity, empathy, and courage contributes to a narrative of connection and purpose. Whether through the relationships we nurture, the insights we share, or the values we embody, our perspective becomes a gift to those we touch.

Applying Perspective in Everyday Life

As we conclude this journey, the question arises: how do we carry these lessons forward? The answer lies in small, consistent actions. Perspective is not something we acquire once and for all; it is a practice that unfolds in the choices we make each day.

Start by cultivating clarity in your own life. Take time to reflect on your values, priorities, and aspirations. Simplify where you can, focusing on what truly matters. Embrace mindfulness and intentionality, allowing each moment to guide you toward a deeper understanding.

Next, engage with the world around you. Challenge assumptions, seek diverse perspectives, and approach others with empathy. Practice curiosity and humility, recognizing that each interaction is an opportunity to learn and grow.

Finally, consider the legacy you wish to leave. Reflect on how your perspective shapes your relationships, contributions, and impact. Whether through mentorship, storytelling, or acts of service, find ways to share your insights and inspire others.

A Final Reflection

Perspective is not a destination but a journey—a lifelong practice of seeing, learning, and growing. It invites us to approach life with curiosity, courage, and compassion, finding meaning in both the extraordinary and the everyday.

As we step forward, let us carry the lessons of this journey with us, not as rigid rules but as guiding principles. Let us embrace the complexities of life with an open heart and mind, trusting that each challenge and triumph adds depth to our understanding. And let us remember that the art of perspective is, above all, an act of hope—a belief in our capacity to grow, connect, and create a better world.

In the words of the poet Mary Oliver: *"What will you do with your one wild and precious life?"* The answer lies in the perspective you cultivate, the choices you make, and the legacy you leave. May your journey be one of clarity, purpose, and inspiration, enriching not only your own life but also the lives of those you touch.

ACKNOWLEDGEMENT

This book would not have been possible without the encouragement, inspiration, and guidance of so many remarkable individuals.

To my family and close friends, your unwavering support and belief in my work have been a source of strength and motivation. Your love and understanding gave me the space and clarity needed to embark on this journey.

To the thinkers, writers, and philosophers whose ideas have stood the test of time, thank you for providing a foundation of wisdom that shaped the themes and narratives of this book. Your insights continue to illuminate the path toward clarity and understanding.

To my readers, both new and returning, your curiosity and commitment to personal growth inspire me to write with purpose and heart. This book was created with you in mind, and it is my hope that its lessons resonate and empower you on your journey.

Finally, to the moments of challenge and uncertainty that prompted reflection and growth, thank you for teaching me the value of perspective.

With gratitude,
Felix Grayson

ABOUT THE AUTHOR

 Felix Grayson's journey into timeless wisdom began in childhood, captivated by the stories of philosophers, leaders, and visionaries who shaped the way we think and live. Growing up in a home filled with books, he spent countless hours exploring ideas that asked life's biggest questions—a curiosity that would later define his work.

After facing his own modern challenges—balancing ambition, uncertainty, and the search for meaning — Felix discovered that the wisdom of the past offers profound guidance for the present. This realization became the foundation for the *Stoned Philosopher* series: a collection dedicated to translating ancient insights into practical lessons for today's world.

Felix's writing is more than reflection — it's an invitation to dialogue with history's greatest minds. Through each book, he helps readers find clarity, resilience, and purpose in their own lives — one timeless idea at a time.

When not writing, Felix enjoys quiet contemplation, deep conversation, and exploring the endless pursuit of wisdom in everyday moments.